Becoming an Effective Classroom Manager

BECOMING AN EFFECTIVE CLASSROOM MANAGER

A Resource for Teachers

Bob F. Steere

State University of New York Press

Published by
State University of New York Press, Albany

©1988   State University of New York

For information, address State University of New York
Press, State University Plaza, Albany, N.Y., 12246

Library of Congress Cataloging in Publication Data

Steere, Bob F., 1931-
    Becoming an effective classroom manager.

    Bibliography: p.
    Includes index.
    1. Classroom management.   2. School discipline—
United States.   I. Title.
LB3013.S657   1988   371.1'024   87-9907
ISBN 0-88706-620-8
ISBN 0-88706-621-6 (pbk.)

10 9 8 7 6 5 4 3 2 1

Contents

Preface

To meet the demands of today's classroom, it is not enough for institutions of higher learning to produce teachers who know their subject and follow good teaching methods. These two pedagogic traits are useless unless the graduates can maintain an orderly, well-managed classroom. This book advocates the use of a multi-faceted approach when training and inservicing teachers in classroom management procedures. The three primary subjects discussed are learning managerial and instructional methods that tend to prevent discipline problems, learning how to spontaneously cope with management problems through the use of desist techniques, and learning how to solve managerial problems.

Teachers proficient in only one facet of classroom management are more susceptable to both stress and failure. For example, it is not enough to be proficient in pedagogy, for the proficient teacher has no insurance against managerial problems. A teacher may be proficient in employing instructional skills but be inefficient in producing student learning—if students are not consistently on worthy tasks. Likewise, a high profile, rough instructor may temporarily make students subservient to her commands, but even more appropriate desist techniques are frequently short-lived in effectiveness. The third facet of solving managerial problems is another valuable and complex skill, but constraints on instructional time limits the time that a teacher can devote to problem solving. Little achievement will be forthcoming from students if their instructional leader must spend excessive instructional time solving managerial problems.

In summary, public school teachers of this era must know appropriate managerial and instructional methods and be preventers of discipline problems. They must be professionals who not only know how to prevent most problems, but who can also analyze situations and then employ either an established approach or develop a personalized, eclectic plan for improving the situation and for preventing its recurrence. But even possession of these skills is not enough. Teachers must be able to use their management techniques while maintaining an environment conducive to learning. Thus the emphasis of this book is on *effective maintenance of classrooms that are conducive to learning.*

The chapters which follow will verify this commitment as the reader is exposed to a variety of management models, research proven approaches, managerial methods offered by successful teachers, and techniques for preventing and correcting routine and unique classroom problems. The teachings of this book will be fused and further modeled in the Appendices in the form of thirty-three innovative managerial activities that have been proven effective by successful classroom managers.

Acknowledgments

My gratitude is expressed to Shirley Jiles for deciphering and typing the initial copy, and to Kathleen Grim for the typing of the final manuscript.

To Pat Hensley goes my sincere appreciation for her editing of the initial manuscript.

And, thank you, Loretta and students, for your encouragement.

Part I

Introduction and Management Models

1

A Portrayal of School Discipline

One reason for the popularity and frequent adoption of the Assertive Discipline Model is that it emphasizes the conclusions emerging from studies of school crime and violence—namely, that school conduct and safety depend to a large extent on teachers and schools having clearly stated rules and consequences for violation of the stated rules. Approaches as obvious as this, as well as other, more structured managerial policies and methods, are ways in which we hope to make schools both safer and more effective as learning centers.

A few misbehaving youths can impede the learning opportunities for receptive students, and more than a few disruptive children "make education virtually impossible." (Bauer, 1985, p. 488). With this truth in mind, many schools are becoming more insistent that all students be accountable for their behavior—that a few will not be allowed to disrupt the learning of many. In the sixties and seventies, educators relaxed the standards of accountability which had been previously imposed upon each student. During these decades, when the teachings of the humanists flourished, we found someone or something to blame for social problems. When children became disruptive or violent, we frequently reasoned that they were victims of unfortunate circumstances and therefore were not to be held accountable for their actions. They were thought to be victims of society and were treated as such (Bauer, 1985, p. 489). Today's educators still recognize the influences of the home and society on the student but increasingly are less accepting of unfortunate personal factors as justifiable excuses for hurting or depriving others of opportunities.

Has the attitudinal change toward "being responsible for one's actions" resulted in youth being more, or less, disciplined? Are

3

crime and violence in the schools running rampant, and are the presence and intensity of this violence severe enough to warrant intervention by state politicians, lawyers, the United States Departments of Education and Justice, and the president of the United States? President Reagan summarized his concern and those of many in his February, 1984, speech to secondary school principals: "I can't say it too forcefully: to get learning back into our schools, we must get crime and violence out" (Sawyer, 1983). The president's concern is seemingly fortified by Rutter's 1979 study of inner-city schools in London, where "students who transferred from behaviorally 'bad' elementary schools to 'good' secondary schools became good students and vice versa" (Baker, 1985, p. 483).

The concerns of individuals and groups about school violence and crime have prompted the creation of the National School Safety Center (NSSC), whose purpose is to "serve the entire nation as a central resource by providing computerized school safety clearinghouse and counseling services" (Sawyer, 1983). The goal of the center is to restore safety in the schools by providing leadership and direction in reducing crime on campuses. School safety requires more than the mere addition of security personnel, ten-foot-high fences, and bigger locks. The center invites a cooperative effort by educators, parents, and concerned citizens—including lawyers and judges. It is encouraging our country's 625,000 lawyers and 24,000 judges to become more involved in education by promoting preventive legal programs rather than by increasing litigation. Examples of the center's preventive measures are offered in *School Safety and the Legal Community* (NSSC, 1985).

Although it is as much corrective as preventive and although it is not an outgrowth of school violence, one innovative approach for dealing with teenager misdemeanors is the Odessa Texas Teen Court Program. The teen court is supervised, but the lawyers, judge, jury, bailiffs, and clerks are youth who were once defendants. Each participating defendant must plead guilty, understand that his or her sentence will require jury duty and community service, and be accompanied in court by parents who will attend a workshop on behavior modification techniques. By serving on juries, the youth become a responsible part of the judicial system—a role that requires some analytical thinking about misbehavior and the rights of others. The Odessa system has dealt with one thousand cases in a year, and appears to be successful. "Thus far, no teenager found guilty of a misdemeanor and fewer than 15 percent of traffic offenders have been in further trouble" (Weiner, 1985, p. 4).

Politicians' concern over violence in the schools have resulted in legislation ranging from reforms requiring improved disciplinary programs to more specific actions designed to curtail drug trafficking. California is one of these states, and its governor, in 1984, signed a package of bills which required standardized reporting of school crime, increased the penalties for campus crimes, and required the courts to notify the schools of students who have committed violent crimes. More states, especially since the president has expressed his interest in safer schools, are following California's initiative. "Since January 1984, 11 states have acted on school discipline legislation; 14 states have formed task forces on school discipline and crime" (Bauer, 1985, p. 490).

In addition to the concerns being shown by interest groups and state and national leaders, the Gallup Organization's perennial polls consistently find respondents most frequently citing discipline as the top problem with which schools must contend. Although this finding is true for all years except two between 1969 and 1986, those with children in public schools mentioned this problem significantly less often in 1984 than in 1983. The 1983 poll found 29 percent of the respondents naming discipline as the biggest problem, whereas only 23 percent mentioned it in the 1984 survey (Gallup, 1984, p. 36). This downward trend has continued, as is evidenced by the 1986 Gallup poll (1986, p. 44), which cited drugs (28 percent) as the public's top concern and discipline as the second most important problem confronting the schools.

Are there any data to justify this concern about violence and disciplinary problems in the schools? DePrete's 1981 study shows a definite relationship between the grades and the behavior of sophomores (see table 1.1; Baker, 1985, p. 483). Not surprisingly, students who regularly consume alcohol are also found to have lower grades. Although it is difficult to believe, Noble (1978) reports that a survey of students in grades seven through twelve found 19 percent of the respondents to be problem drinkers and 60 percent of the high school seniors to have used illicit drugs.

TABLE 1.1 *Relationship Between Grades and Behavior*

Misbehavior	Mostly As	Mostly Bs	Mostly Cs	Mostly Ds
Average days absent per semester	2.28	2.99	4.20	7.87
Average days late per semester	2.05	3.12	4.41	6.44
Percentage of sample not doing assigned homework	1.10	2.73	6.27	24.72
Percentage of sample who cut a class during the school year	28.73	43.39	58.15	67.12
Percentage of sample who have been in serious trouble with the law	1.62	2.93	7.37	14.06

Students are the most frequent victims of crimes committed on campuses. To lose one's personal belongings or to be physically threatened or attacked are indeed tragedies, but they may be lesser ones than the resulting attitude that is developed by the victims. The child who is abused in some manner is likely to become less respectful of the personnel and place where the abusive act occurred. When the place is a school, the victim may learn to feel unsafe there, a feeling which results in reduced attendance and attentiveness and lower grades.

The Safe School Study (1978), though now dated, gives an idea of the types and numbers of unlawful acts occurring in secondary schools. In each month of 1978, 2.4 million students had property stolen, 112,000 of these students were robbed by force, and more than 380,000 students were physically attacked. The Safe Schools Commission (1983) of Boston, as reported by James Fox (cited in Baker, 1985, p. 486), found that 38 percent of high school students had been victims of theft or had been assaulted at least once during the previous year.

Teachers are also victims of aggressive acts. The Safe School Study found that each month six thousand teachers were robbed and one thousand teachers received medical attention as a result of being assaulted. A survey conducted by the *Detroit Free Press* found that "one out of five teachers had been assaulted by a student, and three out of 100 had been assaulted by a parent" (cited in Bauer, 1985, p. 490). With these findings it is easy to believe those of the Metropolitan Life survey (Harris, 1984), which found that 95 percent of our teachers believed school discipline and safety should be given a much higher priority.

The appropriate response to the questions posed earlier, is school violence running rampant and are youth less disciplined, would seemingly be answered with a resounding "yes"—if answered in accordance with the studies cited. But if such findings are truly descriptive and the portrait accurate, it is difficult to understand why anyone would enter or remain in the teaching profession.

Frederic Jones believes, as do many, that violence as reported by the press and in the above paragraphs inappropriately stereotypes students' misbehavior in our schools.

> During thousands of systematic classroom observations in inner-city and suburban elementary and secondary schools, we rarely observed extreme outbursts of fighting or children running berserk around the room. What we found was not a blackboard jungle, but rather massive time wasting (Jones, 1979, p. 27).

Although many novice teachers fear crises, it is the innocuous talking and wandering around the room which accounts for 90 to 99 percent of the classroom disruptions. A National Education Association (NEA) poll (1983) found that approximately 15 percent of the teachers felt that misbehavior interfered with their teaching to a *great* extent—and that discipline problems and teacher stress were not limited to secondary teachers. The survey found that elementary teachers suffer more interference due to student misbehavior than do high school teachers, but that high school students commit more criminal acts. Baker (1985) makes an interesting interpretation of why misbehaving high schoolers interfere less with the teachers' efforts than do the elementary school students. He suggests that many high school teachers and their uninterested or troublesome students have compromised. The students are allowed to ignore the teachers' instructional efforts if they do not disrupt the class. By contrast, more elementary teachers insist that all students pay attention, and consequently" elementary

7

teachers face a more persistent battle with disruptive students"
(pp. 484-485).

The studies cited earlier and other related publications suggest
that the most frequently reported crime on our campuses—theft—
is declining, that the number of attempted assaults is remaining
stable, and that there is a slight decline in the number of teachers
who feel that misbehaving students moderately or greatly interfere
with their teaching. And what is the updated status of drugs in our
secondary schools? Information released during March of 1985 by
the Office of Health and Human Services acknowledges that alcohol and marijuana usage may be declining but that the use of
cocaine is rising in our schools because of reduced costs. The Office
of Health and Human Services quoted a 1984 survey conducted by
the University of Michigan Institute for Social Research showing
that 5 percent of high school seniors are daily users of alcohol
compared with 7 percent in 1979. As to the daily use of marijuana,
5 percent of the seniors are daily users compared with 11 percent
in 1978 (*Joplin Globe*, March 21, 1985, p. 8B). Two especially
depressing findings are that about one in six 13-year-olds has used
marijuana, and that cocaine is readily available in a cheap potent
form called "crack." Crack is more affordable to new users—
including elementary school students (U.S. Department of Education, 1986). A 1985 survey by the National Institute on Drug Abuse
verified the increased use of cocaine, and that the number of marijuana users had dropped between 1982 and 1985 (*Education
Week*, October 22, 1986, p. 2).

How successful have schools, parents, and societal groups been
in combating the use of drugs? Overall, we have been ineffectual.
Bonnie Bernard and her coauthors (1987) found that drug education in the late 1960s was centered on giving information. This
highly cognitive approach gave way in the mid-1970s to one which
focused on affective strategies and the potential user's life skills of
decision making, coping, and problem solving. The late 1970s
found drug education focusing on both cognitive and affective
components—but substance use did not decline. Nevertheless,
although past drug education has resulted in discouraging outcomes, analyses of the past programs have also shown educators
the flaws that need to be corrected in upgrading future programs
such as the "social psychological model"—a newer program "which

appears to be producing good results" (Bernard, Fagoglia, and Perone, 1987, p. 2).

Although this state of affairs is of little comfort, many practicing educators, students, and opinion polls acknowledge an improved attitude among our youth in how they react to authority and rules of conduct (Wayson, 1985, p. 129). Apparently, the more anti-establishment, existentialistic youth of the 1970s have been replaced in the 1980s with more respectful counterparts who are more receptive to societal and institutional standards of conduct.

The data resulting from the aforementioned surveys paint a melancholy portrait of school conduct. But the picture perceived by many citizens, politicians, and teachers is tainted by a preconception that schools are jungles with inhabitants void of values, respect for societal laws, and leadership. This, vehemently, is not the case although there is room for improvement. Even though the schools' status as a social institution is considerably improved, their public image will be slow in changing due to fictional television series and the great interest the media has in reporting school violence. Although one act of violence is too many, we should react to these statistics on violent acts only after realizing that there are 13 million secondary schoolchildren and 32 million elementary schoolchildren in the United States.

Thankfully, classroom management is as much a science as it is an art, and therefore it can be taught and learned. Teachers and principals are becoming better trained in using techniques resulting from effective schools research, in learning tested management models, and in accumulating a repertoire of proven methods for preventing and correcting classroom management problems. This book contributes to this general effort.

Questions and Tasks

1. What probably caused educators to relax their disciplinary requirements during the 1960s and 1970s?

2. Is there any evidence to show that "good" or "bad" schools influence children's behavior? Explain.

3. What is the goal of the National School Safety Center?

4. Is the addition of security personnel and bigger locks the

solution to school violence? Explain.

5. What is your opinion of the Odessa Teen Court Program?

6. What does the Gallup survey tell us about school discipline?

7. Is discipline frequently identified as a pressing school problem because the public does not possess enough knowledge about other school problems? Explain your answer.

8. Summarize the findings of DiPrete and Noble.

9. What would you, as a teacher, do if a student told you he or she had been "shook down," or threatened?

10. What is your reaction to "One out of five teachers had been assaulted by a student, and three out of 100 had been assaulted by a parent"?

11. Did Frederic Jones find schools to be "blackboard jungles"?

12. What is Baker's rationale as to why misbehaving high schoolers interfere less with the teachers' efforts than do the elementary school students?

13. According to the Office of Health and Human Services, is the use of alcohol and marijuana increasing or declining?

14. Summary questions: What is the current status of violence and discipline problems in schools today as compared with that of the past? Can school discipline be improved? How?

2

Classroom Management Approaches

Measures of force

Educators, psychologists, and sociologists advocate numerous models, approaches, theories, procedures, and recipes for teachers to use when confronted with classroom management problems— so many, in fact, that the techniques tend to overlap, to be eclectic combinations of each other, and to be so numerous that it is not feasible to attempt a comprehensive study of them. But an overview of several will provide a foundation for analyzing your beliefs about management theories and practices, serve as building blocks in developing your own personal classroom management system, and help you conceptualize the content of the related chapters.

Classrooms are largely managed by forceful efforts, some of which are less obvious than others. *Force* is defined here as the energy that is brought to bear upon a situation. The management systems presented in the following chapters are ranked according to the comparative amount of personal and professional energy that is needed to develop, implement, and maintain them.

The phrase *teacher force*, as used in these chapters, might seem to imply that the use of more force means that the teacher is an undesirable authoritarian, or that teachers who use more force must be having difficulty keeping their classes under control. But neither of these interpretations is correct. Rather, the phase means (1) that some degree of force (at least organizational structure) is employed by all managers and management styles (models), (2) that different management models employ varying amounts of force, and (3) that force is expressed in different ways.

11

The first idea, that classrooms are largely managed by force, is supported by the fact that force is being exerted whenever a system imposes regulatory pressures upon its clients. This is true whether the regulation calls for punctuality, honesty, quietness, or participation. Any requirement forced upon people is a forceful act.

The second basic idea—that management models employ varying amounts of force—may appear to be the most self-evident of the three. However, it is not so obvious, especially if one considers covert management acts. For example, managerial force may be used to get a client to talk about himself or herself while simultaneously and consciously refraining from condemning the client's unsocial behavior. Both of these behaviors involve the expenditure of energy, even though they are not as readily recognizable as more overt forceful acts, as when a teacher uses a frown, issues a directive, gives a sarcastic statement, issues a positive reinforcer, or administers corporal punishment. Furthermore, force can bring about acts that are perceived as being either positive (as when a teacher records a point which gives a child free time) or negative (as when it becomes necessary to isolate a child from his or her peers).

The third basis for believing that classrooms are largely managed by force is the belief that force is used in different ways. For example, a noncritical observer may not detect a teacher using forceful behavior in a well-managed classroom, but, upon looking more closely, may detect the frequent use of body language that communicates specific requirements and demands to students. In interviewing the same teacher later, the observer may learn that a greater degree of *overt* force was used in initially developing and shaping desirable behaviors during the first weeks of school, whereas now primarily a *covert* force is used in maintaining the learning environment.

The various management models presented in this book have been ranked according to estimates of their relative amounts of structure imposed upon students and their associative forces—the total energy expended in getting students to exhibit socially acceptable behavior. This ranking is illustrated by comparing "Counseling" and "Jones's Management Approach." Indirect counseling imposes very little structure and force upon clients, whereas Jones's model imposes considerable direct force and energy in forcing student compliance. The models also vary in their degree of completeness. Some only encompass preventive concepts (Maslow's

Hierarchy of Needs), others are primarily used in assisting students to improve (Counseling), and others are designed as intervention models (Glasser's Reality Therapy).

Counseling
Ginott's Congruent Communication
Maslow's Need Hierarchy
Values and Morality
Transactional Analysis
Dreikurs' Mistaken Goal
Glasser's Reality Therapy
Contingency Management
Assertive Discipline
Jones's Management Approach

Although the approaches are incomplete models and most do not provide step-by-step procedures, they all contribute to one's development of a personalized management system. That all of them are accepted in varying degrees by learned educators and that each has enjoyed some degree of success in regulating the behavior of pupils, shows, if nothing else, the incredible flexibility of youth in adjusting to the regulatory whims of adults. Such an extreme variety of models must also suggest that almost any procedure designed to change behavior, if designed and implemented with empathy, professionalism, and expertise, will produce desirable results.

Analyzing the models

Each of the following chapters will give you a chance to identify the variables associated with a given model. First, at the end of each discussion is a list of the "measures of force" needed to implement the system. As a critical reader, you will probably be able to identify additional measures of force that might be needed. Second, you will undoubtedly weigh the system's advantages and disadvantages— that is, you will consider the value of each system. These estimates of worth may be of a personal nature: for example, you might decide that a system is too authoritarian for your personality. You might also value a system because research supports its effectiveness, or you may not value it because it is not complete enough or because you believe yourself to be too inconsistent a person to be able to enforce its rules. You can analyze the measures of force needed and the value of each system by making the following chart:

FIGURE 2.1 *Force-field and value analysis chart.*

Forces Involved in the System	Values of the System (Positive and Negative)
•	•
•	•
•	•
•	•
•	•
•	•

In the left-hand column, list all the forces used (energy expended) in both developing and maintaining the system.

In the right-hand column, list all the values of the system: both its positive and negative attributes.

Now, rank the variables in each column from most important to least important.

Analyze each column: first the forces, then the values.

- What do your rankings tell you about yourself?
- Can you muster enough energy and consistency to successfully develop and implement the chosen managerial system?
- Do the positive values outweigh the negative ones?
- What can you do to overcome and become more positive toward the undesired forces and values listed under both columns?
- Can the system be modified in such a way that it becomes acceptable to you without the change contradicting the underlying beliefs and practices of the system?

Creating your own classroom management system

As you study the various managerial approaches, it will become evident that various writers believe that their model, in its pure state, is the correct one for managing behavior in the classroom, but, thankfully, classroom teachers are not compelled to rigidly commit themselves to one construct. Rather, teachers may modify a model, fuse two or more, or develop their own managerial procedures to produce an eclective, personalized model that has little obvious relation to any of the given models.

Regardless of the management model adopted or developed, both experienced and beginning teachers will on occasion find it inadequate. This will be true whether the procedural model was developed from generalities found in child psychology and theoretical management models, or from a course of study which provided specific procedures for dealing with specific problems. Since there is a limitless range of children's behaviors, one approach will not work for all children in all situations.

If you unequivocally feel that a particular model best satisfies your managerial needs, you might wonder whether it is necessary to become acquainted with other models and methods of regulating individuals' and group behaviors. The answer is that teachers should be more than technicians, more than persons skilled in employing one method well. Rather, they should be professionals—individuals who know many managerials alternatives, know of the likely consequences which will result when a chosen procedure is employed, and be responsible for deciding which procedure to use. Even if you fully accept one of these systems, you must fuse it and make it compatible with your own personality and instructional methods. Even then you must consider and develop alternative strategies, since no system can prescribe how to prevent and correct all management problems.

Consider the following three recommendations in developing your own management system.

1. Adopt a system as a basis for developing your own system. Don't go into the classroom thinking that "things will work out"—that a planned management system is unnecessary and too structured for you and your philosophy of teaching.

2. Modify the adopted system to your style to the degree that it remains free of inconsistencies. For example, you may decide that you need more than a few rules in using the Assertive Discipline approach. If that is your choice, then you must be able to consistently enforce the larger number of rules.

3. Make the system more complete by adding needed preventive and corrective techniques. For instance, since Canters' Assertive Discipline does not speak directly to the handling of excuses

offered by students for their misbehavior, how will you discourage excuses and make students responsible for their behavior? This and other such questions will be dealt with in Parts II and III of this book.

To sum up, it behooves you to study the descriptions of the various managerial approaches in the upcoming chapters with the purpose of conceptualizing the content of each, visualizing yourself using the procedures advocated in the approaches, and deciding which parts of the system have questionable value and which parts hold greater promise for use in your future classroom. In picturing yourself using a model, consider your personality in relation to the amount of energy that must be expended in effectively developing, implementing, and maintaining the system. An adopted managerial model will wear better if its procedures are compatible with your normal behaviors. But remember: what is easiest is not necessarily the best. Sometimes it is more efficient to spend an exorbitant amount of energy initially or to choose a less natural approach in order to achieve greater success. By critically reviewing the "measures of force" associated with each approach, you will have reviewed the primary forces and changes required of you—your unique self—in successfully implementing each model.

It bears repeating once again that these models are seldom practiced exactly as described—we become eclectic in developing our personalized management systems, and teachers must remain flexible after implementing a management system because classroom behavior is directly linked to a teacher's methods. The importance of selecting appropriate methods and remaining flexible was summarized by Harry Wong. Mr. Wong (1986), master teacher and lecturer on teaching effectiveness, reminds us that "if we do what we have been doing, we will continue to get what we have been getting."

Management Models

Counseling

Nondirect counseling. People often solve their problems by telling them to a professional listener. Psychiatrists serve as professional listeners, and so too can school counselors and teachers. Professional listeners listen in a reflective way to the troubled person's feelings, patiently waits for the client to continue discussing his behavior or problem, and then repeats the client's feelings when the expressions cease.

Because the listener remains noncritical, nonjudgmental, warm, and empathetic, the student tends to bring forth buried feelings and to more truthfully evaluate the problem. When students pour out their problems to a listener, they then know what to do about them. Naturally, this is not true if they have not developed an appropriate value system and are intellectually incapable of synthesizing appropriate solutions. With young children it is sometimes necessary to become "less indirect" in finding solutions.

Professional listening is harder than it appears. It is difficult to not volunteer a surefire simple plan that, if practiced by the child, would make his or her life much more pleasant while also making all involved adults ecstatic. But the professional listener must remain nonjudgmental, listen with an honest attempt to understand, and hear not only what the child is saying but also what he or she is trying to say.

Some students will single out a teacher to be their counselor even though they are not in that teacher's class. One reason for this behavior was well expressed by Brenda Ueland in 1941.

Who are the people . . . to whom you go for advice? Not to the hard practical ones who can tell you exactly what to do, but to the listeners; that is, the kindest, least censorious, least bossy people that you know. It is because by pouring out your problems to them, you then know what to do about it yourself . . . (cited in Wallen and Wallen, 1978, p. 277).

The nondirective counselor, while not being censorious, should be able to keep the conversation going and focused on the student's problem. This technique most frequently involves the use of *repetition* and *clarification*, as illustrated in figure 2.2.

FIGURE 2.2 *Counseling Technique*

Technique		Dialogue
	Kari	(Crying) No one likes me.
Repeat . .	Teacher	(Waits three to five seconds, or until it becomes obvious Kari will not continue.) You think that no one likes you.
	Kari	Yes. I don't have any friends.
Repeat . .	Teacher	(Waits three to five seconds, or until it becomes obvious Kari will not continue.) You say that you have no friends.
Clarification	Kari	Uh, huh!
. . . .	Teacher	(Waits three to five seconds, or until it becomes obvious Kari will not continue.) Why do you think you have no friends?
	Kari	Because no one will play with me.

(C. Rogers, in Wallen and Wallen, 1978, p. 278)

Another way to ask for clarification, other than asking a "why" question, is to ask for an example: "Tell me about the time when someone showed she didn't like you." The counselor's objective is to keep the conversation going in order to allow buried concerns to surface, to allow the student to explore his or her feelings, and to hopefully allow the student to bring forth a feasible solution to the problem. Everything, be it a handmade craft or a plan of action, is usually better remembered and more internalized if it is developed by oneself.

Direct counseling. In the direct approach, the counselor is more forthright in helping students view their behavior in light of how it affects themselves, others, and society, and in making them more aware of alternative ways of behaving and coping.Some young people apparently are unable to view themselves and their behavior through the eyes of those with whom they interact. To enlighten them, "enlightening counselors" usually start the conference by having the students describe the incident; during this description, the counselors express sympathy for the students' feelings. Talking about the incident to an unemotional listener will make a youth less stressed, more rational, and therefore more receptive to suggested alternative and coping behaviors.

The counselor will ultimately say to the student, "Let's try to think of some things which would work better should a similar situation arise." Here the counselor's objective is to provide the youth with alternative behaviors. Carl and LaDonna Wallen note that a teacher's success in carrying out the strategy of enlightenment requires the teacher to "(1) be factual and unemotional; (2) emphasize the what rather than the why; and (3) offer indirect suggestions by prefacing each with statements such as 'I wonder whether . . .?' 'Could it be that . . .?' 'Something you might want to try that has worked for other students is . . .' " (1978, pp. 288-289).

Measures of Force Involved in Counseling
Energy exerted in the following: Making the environment conducive to counseling. Consciously remaining a counselor, that is, critical, warm, empathetic, etc. Becoming an enlightening counselor during direct counseling sessions.

Ginott's congruent communication

Haim Ginott, former professor of psychotherapy and resident psychologist of television's *Today Show*, viewed discipline as a series of little victories, as a long-term developmental process, and as an immediate solution to a child's misbehavior (Charles, 1983, pp. 56-57). He believed that teachers should be gentle persuaders that use calm language which appropriately fits situations and feelings—that they should use "congruent communications." Teachers should also find alternatives to punishment because a punished child is not very educable. Punishment often results in grudges, hostility, emotional distress, and thoughts of vengeance.

Ginott's model for correcting children's behavior is largely based on the words spoken to students when "teachers are at their worst" and when "teachers are at their best." Teachers at their *worst* are sarcastic, attack students' character, label them, and serve as poor models of human behavior. Teachers at their *best* accept and acknowledge feelings, avoid sarcasm and labeling, invite cooperation, and address the problem rather than the pupil's personality. When correcting a student, tell or show them what behavior is expected of them by speaking to the situation and not by judging the child's character.

Ginott believed that teachers should handle conflicts calmly without losing their tempers. There will be times when a teacher is upset, and this hurt can be expressed as displeasure by the use of an "I-message" such as "I am disappointed." This approach is more appropriate than the use of "you-messages" that shame students with sentences like "You're lazy and disrespectful." The use of I-messages is also a characteristic of Thomas Gordan's (1974) management model identified as TET—teacher effectiveness training. Another similarity links Ginott's system with both TET and Roger's client-centered therapy. All three emphasize feeding back to the chid his or her feelings rather than analyzing the message's content. All three advocate conveying empathy and helping the troubled person find his or her own solutions.

Ginott's model reveals the progressive philosophy of the 1960s and early 1970s in that it advocates providing opportunities for children to become less dependent on teachers for education and to become more responsible for what happens in the classroom. For example, a teacher might offer several solutions to a problem and then allow the class to adopt the proper solution. Charles (1983, p. 58) points out that Ginott's procedures do not provide a method of dealing with disrespectful, defiant, and highly disruptive students and therefore are not a complete classroom management model.

Measures of Force Involved in Ginott's Congruent Communication
Energy exerted in the following: Developing calm language which appropriately fits situations and feelings. Finding alternatives to punishment. Preventing oneself from judging a child's character while remaining a good model. Training oneself to use "I" messages rather than "You" messages.

Maslow's hierarchy of needs

Abraham Maslow's pyramidal model (1970) is another approach to understanding behavior. Maslow suggests that humans have needs and qualities that serve as motivators of behavior. His scheme suggests that lower-level needs must be satisfied to a reasonable degree before the more advanced need levels emerge as behavioral motivators. For instance, at the base are *physical needs* and survival, which motivate us to strive for food, clothing, and shelter. An application of Maslow's teachings would point out the fact that a hungry child will not be motivated toward learning long division because his or her mind is on food and a growling stomach. When there is a large hiatus between the learner's needs and the learning objectives of the teacher, then discipline problems may develop.

The second plank of the pyramid is the need for *security and safety*. An abused child or one from a family about to splinter will be concerned with loss of security and the need to find and regain a sense of safety and security. This student, regardless of age, has little motivation for learning—for gaining knowledge.

Once children fulfill their physical, security, and safety needs, they have the need for *love and belonging*. They feel that they have fulfilled this need when they are accepted by others, given attention and affection. After love and belonging comes the need for *respect and self-esteem*. This need is satisfied by having successful accomplishments, by gaining influence and status in groups, and by receiving recognition.

Once the four lower needs are fulfilled, children become less concerned about maintenance needs and become more interested in growth needs—in becoming more *self-actualized* persons. This need is realized by fulfilling one's potential by doing what one is suited to do or wants to do. Such self-fulfilled individuals possess a value system which is influence little by the taste of others.

FIGURE 2.3 *Pyramidal model of needs.*

In moving towards self-actualization, individuals become motivated to better understand and gain knowledge about their world and its processes. They seek knowledge from an intrinsic drive, and find that external payoffs are not required in order to enjoy learning. Likewise, they are intrinsically motivated to become appreciative of order and beauty and to enjoy them both as a creator and, vicariously, as an onlooker. Again, Maslow's hierarchy of needs reminds the classroom manager that scholarly social behavior will be maintained only if basic maintenance needs are first fulfilled. To ignore this concept is to invite conflicts between the teacher's desires and the students' needs. Duke (1986) voices the same principle:

> In schools like Palatine, however, it would be fruitless to dwell on academics until care first had been taken to build relationships with students. It could require several months to do so, but the alternative was to try to. *force* students to learn. Many of Palatine's students came to school feeling so unsure of their own abilities and so distrustful of adults that their ability to benefit from instruction was seriously impaired. It would have been a waste of time for teachers to plunge into academic work without taking time to get to know students and vice versa (Duke, 1986, pp. 30-31).

Duke undoubtedly agrees with Maslow that learning is unlikely to occur until a child feels accepted and respected by the teacher and at least some classmates.

Maslow's work is challanged by exceptions to his hierarchy (Fernald and Fernald, 1978, p. 314). The hungry painter who continues to work without the necessary compensation to adequately fulfill basic physical needs exemplifies an exception, as does the hero or heroine who forgoes the need for safety to save a loved one. Although this model, like the others, is not without fault, the wise teacher must acknowledge the likelihood that discipline problems will result when a teacher pushes a student to value and fulfill learning requirements (knowledge level) when the student has not fulfilled other needs such as food (physical need).

Measures of Force Involved in Maslow's Needs Hierarchy

Energy exerted in the following:

Changing one's attitudes and practices which falesly support the view that all students are equally ready for learning.

Analyzing students for their needs deficiencies.

Developing, locating, and implementing methods and materials used in satisfying "maintenance" needs.

Values and morality

Louis Raths's (1978) value clarification model and the moral reasoning model of Lawrence Kohlberg (1985) are two more models that give us an approach to understanding behavior. They are similar in that both recognize that behavior is influenced by a person's basic beliefs and values.

Raths believes that discipline problems often result from one of two conditions: (1) when a child has unclear values or holds values without conviction, and (2) when the child's values are different from those of the supervising parent or teacher. If children have unclear values or values that have not been fully accepted and made a part of their conscience, they may test behaviors not congruent with the behavior advocated by the school's rules and policies. A child's home and community may also use words not permissible by the school, or a child's value system may cause him or her to make an unacceptable response to an authority. This problem was experienced by an Alaskan teacher of Indian children when a misbehaving child refused to look him in the eyes. The act of looking the older person in the eyes was later learned to be an act of disrespect in the child's culture.

It goes without saying that attitudes (beliefs and values) and behaviors are two different things. A belief, if not thought through and internally accepted—free of pressure of an authority—may not result in desirable behavior. Values and societal norms must be held as convictions if the individual is to consistently behave in desirable ways. The degree that one's values and behaviors are congruent with the norms, rules, and laws of society largely determines whether or not one is perceived as a moral person. Teachers should help students become aware of their values by eliciting value statements, by being nonjudgmental of different values, and by asking questions that will help the students assess their values (Rich, 1985, p. 236; Ryan, 1986, p. 230).

Lawrence Kohlberg believes that moral reasoning is developed through six distinct stages, although stage 6 is sometimes fused with stage 5. A person's moral decisions in the advanced stages of morality are judgments resulting from cognitive thinking and are therefore dependent on the person's ability to reason abstractly. Educators must recognize youths' limitations in abstract reasoning and in developing morality beyond the lower, egocentric stages.

The morality of stage one is based on rules imposed by others and is oriented toward punishment and rewards: one should not do something if it results in punishment. Reasoners in this stage are largely egocentric, being unable to consider the perspectives of others (Arbuthnot and Faust, 1981, p. 54). A school's morality is based in part on stage one (punishment morality) (Curwin and Mendler, 1980, p. 104).

Stage 2 might be called the "back scratcher" stage in that individual acts are considered good if they have a positive consequence for the actor. An example is illustrated by "You don't tell on me for cheating and I'll choose you first at recess." Individuals at this stage are still highly egocentric, but they are starting to internalize morality in recognizing that other people have their own needs. Many students reason in this stage. The morality of stage 2 interferes frequently with teachers identifying wrongdoers.

Stage 3 is called the "good boy" stage (Curwin and Mendler, 1980,

p. 102) in that morality is based on pleasing others. A person working from this stage will justify and excuse his deviant acts if the behavior was committed to improve his image and interpersonal relationships. What is morally good is determined largely from an external authority and not from internalized value. Students at this stage rarely misbehave because they desire to please and to gain acceptance. In fact, some will tell the misdeeds of others in the hope of pleasing the teacher. A *school's* morality is based, in part, on stage 3.

Law and order often characterizes stage 4 in that "right is defined as doing one's duty in society and in upholding the established social order" (Arbuthnot and Faust, 1981, p. 60). Morality here includes respect for those in authority, respect for ownership rights, and beginning to see that one's self is important to the success of society. A school's morality is partly based on stage 4.

In stage 5 individuals move from basing their morality on authority to the development of knowing right from wrong regardless of what the system and society advocate. The right of society overshadows the right of cliques and groups. Each individual has rights regardless of sex, status, and race, and therefore the U.S. Constitution is within itself moral. As is the case with adults, there are relatively few adolescents functioning at stage 5.

Individuals of stage 6 have self-chosen principles of belief and conduct that are held without regard to some authority, reward, or punishment. The beliefs of these individuals are appropriate for all humans: these people would never use a fellow human to reach an unjust end, and they believe in the dignity of each and every person. Few individuals—adults or children—reach this stage.

Classroom managers need to understand moral development to better understand others and to better analyze behavior problems. A student who functions above stages 3 and 4 will probably conflict with teachers who are attempting to manage by employing the principles of stages 1, 3, and 4. Likewise, if Beth is morally reasoning at stage 1 and a teacher is using moral reasoning which exceeds Beth's level, there will be little chance of understanding. One might ask two closing questions: Should the teacher use punishment which is understood by Beth or should the teacher counsel Beth and try to help her move to a higher stage of moral reasoning? And, is it wrong for teachers to teach values and morality? Kohlberg gives the following reply:

If schools wish to foster morality, they will have to provide an atmos-
phere in which interpersonal issues are settled on the basis of principle rather than power. They will have to take moral questions
seriously and provide food for thought instead of conventional "right
answers" (Kohlberg and Hersh, 1985, p. 230).

If values are not *taught*, then they are *caught*. It is better that
children learn the core values of justice, equality, and respect for
others from the teachings of loving parents and teachers. Regrettably, too many children are left to "catch" values by watching
television and talking with peers. The values and behaviors learned
from these two latter groups often conflict with the values advocated by parents and teachers.

Measures of Force Involved in Values and Morality
Energy exerted in the following:
Learning about and becoming more tolerant of the different cultural values and behaviors of students
Remaining cognizant that a student's stage of morality may be different from a school's stage
Assisting students in assessing their values by asking questions to elicit thinking about values
Practicing the belief that teaching the *core values* of justice, equality, and respect is not imposing one's narrow value system upon innocent youths
Infusing multicultural knowledge about different groups' values, beliefs, and customs into the curricula
Practicing the belief that children's moral decisions may be faulty because of their inability to abstractly reason and/or because they are unschooled in the values imposed by the school

Transactional analysis

Transactional analysis is an approach to behavior which recognizes three ego states within each school-age child and teacher:
child, parent, and adult. It also recognizes that these ego states vie
for control during confrontations between teachers and students.
A person who knows that everyone has three ego states, each of
which may emerge at any time, is more aware of the fact that a

dialogue between two individuals may result in nine combinations of ego states with varying degrees of compatibility for the two parties involved in the transaction. By being cognizant of our three ego states and by analyzing transactions, we can gain a more conscious control of how we operate with our students and how they operate with us (James and Jongeward, 1976, p. 39).

The *child* ego state develops soon after birth and includes one's feelings and urges for satisfaction. Eric Berne (1972, p. 12), the originator of transactional analysis and the author of the international best-seller *Games People Play*, states that each of us, regardless of age, "carries within a little boy or little girl."

The *parent* state is that part of the ego that is critical, judgmental, and righteous, as well as nurturant. The person's parent state is at the forefront when "he feels, thinks, acts, talks, and responds just as one of his parents did when he was little" (Berne, 1972, p. 11). This state is often first observed when the young child plays at imitating parental behavior, and, as James and Jongeward (1976, p. 39) note, "Sometimes it's a shock to parents to see themselves being played back."

The *adult* stage emerges as the person begins to exert more control over his or her environment and to examine the accuracy of what he or she learned in the parent stage. The adult analyzes all available facts before appraising the environment and behavior. The "adult" teacher's reactions to misbehaviors are not controlled by emotions and retaliatory anger, but by rational reactions to available input and constraint from becoming involved in power struggles. One may better conceptualize Berne's three ego states by reacting to the following recall exercises.

Recall a childhood behavior that you still use in getting something you want. (Child ego state)

Think of some rule or message received from a parent that you now repeat to your children and associates. (Parent ego state)

Recall an incident during which—though emotional—you made a decision based on the fact and not based on urges and emotions. (Adult ego state)

(James and Jongeward, 1976, p. 41)

It seems appropriate for teachers to remain in the adult state when dealing with conflicts, but occasionally it may be beneficial to move into the nurturant and caring role found in the parent state.

Analyze each transaction in the following two dialogues by identifying each statement as being in the child, parent, or adult state. Which one of the two transactions will more quickly result in improved communications and relations, and be least destructive to the learning environment?

Student: (Angrily) Why don't you get after someone else? You're always on my case.

Teacher: If you don't quiet down, you'll receive a zero for today.

Student: Who cares what you do? You'll give me a zero anyway.

Teacher: If you paid more attention to your work and spent less time fooling around, you'd know a lot more.

Student: Bug off. Leave me alone.

Teacher: That's enough! Go to the principal's office right now. You're not to talk to me with disrespect ever again.

OR

Student: (Angrily) Why don't you get after someone else? You're always on my case.

Teacher: You feel I treat you differently. If you like, Jan, we can discuss this later. O.K.?

Student: Talking won't help. Even if we talk you'll fail me.

Teacher: For now we'll continue with the math lesson. Bill, what does this symbol represent?

Student: See, you just ignore me.

Teacher: Jan, I'm sorry that you're upset with me. I would still like for you to share your feeling with me after class. Now, class where should this symbol be placed?

An analysis of the above two dialogues finds the first teacher's discourse to be governed by the parent ego state. Obviously, the relationship will not improve as a result of the teacher's managerial action. The second dialogue reveals a teacher who remains in the rational adult stage—a person who does not become emotionally upset, attempts to keep the instructional program progressing, and recognizes a need to counsel with the student on a one-to-one basis.

Measures of Force Involved in Transactional Analysis
Energy exerted in the following: Gaining a more conscious control of how we operate with our students and how they operate with us Becoming readily able to recognize the three ego states that may emerge in ourselves and in other people at any time Learning and practicing the belief that you, as a teacher, should remain in the adult stage when dealing with conflict

Dreikurs's mistaken goal model

Rudolf Dreikurs has developed an approach to classroom management which advocates democratic procedures in that it allows older children to help establish rules for classroom behavior. Once these rules are established, the consequences of obeying or disobeying them can be determined: good behavior will result in rewards and misbehavior will result in unpleasant consequences. Dreikurs prefers the idea of a consequence to the idea of punishment, and would not recommend the use of physical punishment.

This model recognizes two types of consequences. A *natural consequence* is a result of the student's own behavior and is not influenced by the teacher. For example, a student playing with matches burns himself. The other type of consequence is identified as *logical* in that the resulting response to the behavior is imposed by the teacher. This situation is exemplified by a student who is denied tomorrow's recess because he fought during today's recess. Dreikurs (Dreikurs, Greenwald, and Pepper, 1982, p. 12) advocates the following considerations in using logical consequences:

1. Each consequence should be related to the misbehavior.

2. The child is to be given a choice. "You can either *walk* in the hall or you can use the outside exit to get to the lunchroom. Which do you choose?"

29

3. Safety and danger situations may prevent the use of logical consequences.

4. Logical consequences work best when the child's goal and behavior is "attention getting."

Consequences are best when predetermined, explained to the students, and posted. Ideally, they are not spontaneously and emotionally determined at the time of the incident. The teacher's image should not be one of a punisher, but one who only enforces the predetermined rules and consequences that were established, at least in part, by the class. When a consequence is administered, it is simply the result of a student's decision to break the rule and to receive the consequence. With time, the student will learn to rely on inner control by associating the fact that undesirable behavior consistently results in undesirable consequences. He or she will learn that pestering others during study time will cause isolation, that incomplete work will require homework, and that being tardy will result in making up the time after school.

The underlying belief of this system is that students want to belong and be accepted, that they are able to choose right from wrong behavior, and that they misbehave because they believe it will get them the recognition they seek. Children are like most other people; they want recognition, and, like many adults, they will resort to disturbing behavior to gain a sense of acceptance and recognition. When one wants acceptance and recognition and believes that recognition can be acquired by gaining attention, seeking power, seeking revenge, or displaying inadequacy, one is said to have a "mistaken goal" or belief. These four mistaken goals are usually sought in sequential order (Charles, 1981, p. 99).

Teachers can identify mistaken goals by observing the child's behavior after the behavior is corrected (Dreikurs, Greenwald, and Pepper, 1982, p. 14-31).

Goal	Examples of Behavior
Attention	May stop the behavior and then repeat it, uses charm, is overly sensitive, over eager to please, shows off, is a nuisance in class, etc.

Power   May refuse to stop, argues, must win, is disobedient, refuses to do work, often lies, must be boss, etc.

Revenge   Has more intense behavior, is destructive, hurts others, wants to get even, believes that nobody likes him, etc.

Inadequacy   Withdraws, refuses to participate, feels helpless or stupid, gives up, feels best when left alone, etc.

When a child's mistaken goal is identified, the late Rudolf Dreikurs and his associates believe the teacher should attempt, in a nonthreatening way, to get the student to examine why he or she is exhibiting the undesirable behavior.

Mistaken Goal	*Types of Probing Questions*
Attention	Could it be that you want to keep me busy with you? Could it be that you want me to give you more attention?
Power	Could it be that you want to be in charge? Could it be that you want to show me that you can do what you want?
Revenge	Could it be that you want to hurt me? Could it be that you want to show me how much you hated what I did?
Inadequacy	Could it be that you feel you cannot do the work? Could it be that you do not know the answer and do not want the other students to know?

Through these and similar questions, the teacher will hopefully open up communications, take the initiative away from the child, and possibly develop a cooperative plan for correcting the behavior and abolishing the mistaken goal.

Measures of Force Involved in Dreikurs' Mistaken Goal Model
Energy exerted in the following: Allowing children to help establish rules   Refraining from the use of physical punishment   Developing and using consequences related to misbehavior   Posting and explaining consequences to students   Helping students develop inner control by getting them to realize that consequences are their choices—as determined by their behavior   Working with and counseling students to examine why they are exhibiting the undesirable behavior

Glasser's reality therapy

Another approach to dealing with students is Glasser's reality therapy. Glasser's premise for correcting behavior problems is in sharp contrast to the approaches used by psychoanalysts, educators, and psychologists. The psychoanalyst feels a need to first learn the cause for the misbehavior by studying the person's background. The psychologist and educator are interested in the environmental conditions of the misbehaving individual. In contrast, Glasser's approach advocates little concern for a person's experiences during infancy, social standing, physical attractiveness, and home life. He sees students as rational beings capable of choosing acceptable behavior—they are in charge of their lives and are therefore responsible for both their behavior and the resulting consequences. Glasser expounds on this belief by saying, "People know what they're doing—including crazy people" (1986). The teacher's role in handling misbehavior is that of forcing students to make value judgments about their behaviors, helping them to choose and commit themselves to more acceptable behavior, and accepting no excuses for poor behavior.

Rules are an essential part of Glasser's system. He recommends that reasonable and enforceable rules be cooperatively developed, or at least agreed to. The rules are to be strictly enforced and excuses are not to be accepted. What goes on at home or in the previous teacher's classroom is no basis for excusing a rule violation in your classroom. If a commitment is not lived up to and an excuse is offered, the excuse is not accepted, but a new plan may be developed. The ongoing theme is that when a student has mutually agreed to rules and then chooses misbehavior, then he or she also has chosen a consequence. It is the student's choice—not the teacher's. When rules are no longer needed, they should be discarded.

Glasser (1978) outlines ten steps in dealing with school discipline problems.

1. What am I doing?
2. Is it working? If not, stop doing it.
3. Recognition. (Give the student "the time of day.")
4. What are you doing?
5. Is it against the rules?
6. Work it out. (Make a plan.)
7. Isolate from the class—within the classroom.
8. Out (In-school suspension).
9. Send the student home.
10. Get professional help.

The steps can be explained as follows.

Step 1: Each teacher with a recurring discipline problem should analyze his or her methods. Are you part of the problem?

Step 2: Does your analysis indicate that your approach is working? If not, quit doing it and implement a new system. Be sure to plan your system with the involvement of other affected persons, such as the principal and cooperating teachers.

Step 3: Glasser recognizes this as possibly the most important of the ten steps. Recognize the student in a sincere and personal way. For example, give the student "the time of day" by greeting him or her, using his or her name in a positive way, and sharing an experience—such as a ball game—with the student.

Step 4: When misbehavior occurs, focus on the student's present behavior by asking, "What are you doing?" This is to focus *awareness* on the student's current behavior.

Step 5:   This step is for the purpose of having the student *evaluate* his or her behavior. This can be done by asking, "Is that what you were directed to do?" "Is it against the rules?" or "Is what you're doing helping you and the class?"

Step 6:   Here the teacher and student formulate a plan with an alternative behavior. The plan may also involve logical consequences if it is not adhered to—if the rule is violated. Punishment is not used because it removes responsibility from the student. The plan should be short, simple, and have success built into it. Should the student say, "I won't do it again," do not continue with step 7.

Step 7:   Should the student continue to misbehave, become defiant, or refuse to work out the problem and develop a plan, then he or she should be isolated within the room. The isolated student should remain in your view but not in the view of other class members, and will remain in isolation until ready to cooperatively plan a solution. This step is skipped for junior and senior high school students.

Step 8:   If the elementary child is disruptive in the in-class isolation, he or she is sent either to the principal or to another teacher's well-managed classroom. In this in-school suspension, the child will remain seated and will not be allowed to become involved in activities or dialogue other than to express a wish to work it out with the sending teacher.

Step 9:   Because a school cannot allow a few misbehaving students to keep teachers from teaching and students from learning, in some situations it may be necessary to place a student under the supervision of the parents through the use of out-of-school suspension.

Step 10:   If the school personnel, the parents, and the student are unable to cooperatively develop a suitable plan, it may be necessary to involve other persons, such as social workers, psychologists, or staff members of alternative schools.

Many of the above steps are illustrated in the following example of Glasser's approach.

FIGURE 2.4

EXAMPLE OF GLASSER'S APPROACH

Situation: An off-task student is wandering around the room periodically distracting on-task students.

Teacher: What are you doing?*(Awareness of current behavior.)*

Bill: Nothing. Just looking.

Teacher: Is that what you were directed to do? *(Have student evaluate his behavior.)*

OR

Is what you're doing helping you and the class?

Bill: I'm not the only one not working.

Teacher: Is what you are doing helping you? Is it against the rules? *(Return the discussion to the student's present behavior.)*

Bill: I guess.

Teacher: Good—I Thought you understood *(Reinforcement)*

Do we need a plan to insure that you will remain on task and not bother others? *(Help student develop a plan for which he is responsible for both the contracted behavior and the resulting consequences.)*

THREE OF SEVERAL POSSIBLE RESPONSES

Bill: I know I shouldn't. I'll not walk around and bother others.

End of incident

Bill: You're the boss.

Sit down during a mutually agreed time and develop a short, simple plan with great possibility for sucess.

Obtain a commitment in the form of a handshake or signed contract.

Bill: continues misbehavior, becomes defiant, or refuses to "work it out."

Isolate Bill within the classroom if an elementary child

Send to principal or to in-school suspension facility

May return to the group when he is willing to behave and develop a plan.

Send home or for professional help if child continues to be disruptive to the instructional process.

35

Glasser qualifies his system by recognizing that it will not work well if a student does not want to be in school. Charles (1983, p. 55) points out the near impossibility of dealing with more than one misbehavior at a time when employing the Glasser system. This system also involves a proportionally large amount of teacher time by requiring student responses in the form of value judgments, statements of commitment, and the development of a plan. Unless the teacher sees time as a precious commodity and knows how to move things along, this approach may play havoc with instructional time.

Measures of Force Involved in Glasser's Reality Therapy
Energy exerted in the following: Helping students make value judgments about their behaviors Helping students choose and commit themselves to more acceptable behavior Learning to accept no excuses for poor behavior Cooperatively developing reasonable and enforceable rules Strictly enforcing rules Remaining ready to develop new plans if earlier ones prove unsatisfactory Unemotionally practicing the belief that students choose their consequences Consistently following the ten steps of the system

Contingency management

Teachers who wish to adopt a new classroom management system with a positive approach but only want to consider systems that have been frequently researched and proven effective should study the contingency management and the token economy models. These systems, which have been profusely implemented and tested in both regular and special classrooms since the middle 1960's, have proved their worth in increasing work output and in improving children's behavior.

Contingency management is a direct descendant of B.F. Skinner's teachings and an indirect descendant of Ivan Pavlov's experiments. We recall Pavlov's classical conditioning experiments, during which he used an unconditioned stimulus (no training) in the form of food to produce an unconditioned response (salivation). Pavlov also found that after repeatedly associating a bell with the introduction of food the animal would salivate (conditioned response) when it sensed the noise of the bell (conditioned stimulus). It formed a conditioned link between the two stimuli—the bell and the food. However, the link was found to be impermanent. After repeated trials, without the presence of the unconditioned stimulus (food), the conditioned stimulus (bell) may lose its ability to cause salivation. When this result occurs, the conditioned response has been extinguished (Gardner, 1982, p. 82).

Whereas the classical conditioning of Pavlov begins with a reflex action (salivation or blinking), the instrumental or operant conditioning experiments of behaviorist B.F. Skinner begin with an operant—a behavior the individual can already produce. Skinner's initial operant was the pressing of a lever by an animal. When the operant appeared, the animal was reinforced with food. The consistent issuance of food (reinforcer) each time the operant occurs increases the chance that the operant (reinforced behavior) will reoccur.

The operant model has proved to be extremely useful to psychologists and educators in changing children's behaviors. These behaviorists believe that behavior can be adequately understood as responses to environmental stimuli. They feel that there is relatively little value in knowing what brought on the misbehavior; what is important is knowing what is happening now to perpetuate the misbehavior and what can be done to change it (Wolfgang and Glickman, 1980, pp. 120-124). If speaking out without permission (response) is a problem, then the teacher should determine what follows the misbehavior. The teacher may come to realize that his or her reaction to the misbehavior has not been effective in curbing it and may decide to replace the reaction with a different consequence (stimulus) which will be awarded contingent on a display of desired behavior (response). Skinner (1986, p. 107) reminds teachers that "we learn when what we do has reinforcing consequences. To teach is to arrange such consequences."

Wallen and Wallen (1978, p. 114) state that the phrase *contingency management* refers to the use of *primary reinforcers*, things that directly meet a person's physiological or psychological need." *Token economy* refers to using *secondary* reinforcers, tokens that are redeemable for the primary reinforcers. Contingency management was used by your mother when she insisted that you put your pajamas on and put your toys away before you could have your treat and milk. Token economy is illustrated by workers receiving money or coupons (tokens) which can be traded for primary reinforcers. The term *contingency management* will hereafter be used in this book to include the teacher's contingent use of primary reinforcers that are immediately issued and also the use of secondary reinforcers (tokens) which can be traded later for desired things to reward a student's preferred behavior.

The development and implementation of a contingency management system demands more of a teacher's time than do most management systems. The teacher must thoroughly plan the system, identifying specifically what, how, and when things are to be done. Contingency managers must also be willing to stop spending large amounts of time with misbehaving children. Instead, they must spend more time and energy "catching children being good" and rewarding them for their good behavior, be it related to school or to general conduct. When disruptive students receive the attention that they desire, they are receiving reinforcement for their misbehavior. When a teacher rewards students exhibiting good behavior and ignores a misbehaving youngster, the misbehavior is usually weakened. That is understandable when we acknowledge our desire for recognition and rewards and our disdain for being left out and ignored. Most behavior modifiers recommend that punishment not be an integral part of the contingency system, although some view the ignoring of misbehavior, while rewarding good behavior, to be "subdued punishment."

Rules. Regardless of whether contingency management is used with one student or with the whole class, the target behavior or rule—the specific, reasonable, and observable behavior—must first be identified and communicated to all involved parties. This behavior may be specifically related to "academics" (for example, it may require the completion of two arithmetic worksheets with 90 percent accuracy) or to "conduct" (for example, there will be no talking without the student first raising his or her hand and being acknowledged). A target behavior which requires a remedial reading sophomore to read and comprehend Shaw's *Pygmalion* before the next day's class is not reasonable, nor is a rule which forbids assistance on homework an observable one.

Reinforcers. Reinforcers are the heart of contingency management. Teachers believe themselves to be frequent users of positive reinforcement, but there is little positive correlation between their beliefs and the amount of reinforcement actually dispensed. Contingency managers must carefully consider including four types of reinforcers into their contingency management plan: social, token, activity, and tangible. *Social* reinforcers are commonly used by most people in interacting with each other. A caring touch, smile, tone of voice, and word of praise are all social reinforcers frequently used by teachers. As mentioned earlier, *token* reinforcers are secondary reinforcers which are rewarded for good behavior and which can be collected, saved, and exchanged for primary reinforcers. Tokens may be in the form of points, stars, coupons, stamps, poker chips, checkmarks, money, or punches on a card. *Activity* reinforcers are activities rewarded to students for doing some preferred behavior; examples of these rewards are playing checkers, having five minutes of extra recess, and cleaning the erasers. *Tangible* reinforcers are primary reinforcers exemplified by a Chocolate Kiss candy, a yo yo, and a Michael Jackson stick-on.

Contingency management plans have varying degrees of complexity. The following is a modification of a relatively simple approach described by Wallen and Wallen (1978, p. 114).

> Prepare a large legible chart headed by TASK and which specifically states the tasks to be completed. Prepare another chart entitled REWARD which lists the rewards (reinforcers) for correctly completing the task. The teacher then distributes the assigned work sheets to each child and gives the directions that each child will raise a hand upon completion of the tasks. When the child's hand is raised, the teacher moves to the student and checks the accuracy of the completed assignments. Errors must be corrected. Students with error free work may move to the Reward Area and select an activity. The Reward Period goes on until the last student spends five minutes with a reward activity. The class is then directed to quietly return to the Instructional Area of the classroom.

Although a contingency management system which immediately provides the primary reinforcer (reward) is desirable, it has disadvantages. The last finishers consistently receive the least desired activity, there may be difficulty in managing all students at once in the Reward Area, the activities of the early finishers may disturb the students still working, and students may become impatient when a backlog of papers forces them to wait for the teacher to check their assigned tasks. Needless to say, the teacher's plans should address these potential problems and provide a structure which will prevent them from evolving.

A contingency management plan that employs tokens provides more flexibility than a management plan that provides primary reinforcers, but it also requires more administrative planning. As emphasized earlier, the program must be thoroughly planned and the teacher must consistently adhere to the plan. The planner is obliged to consider the particulars outlined in the next section.

Designing a token contingency management plan.

SPECIFY AND POST THE TARGET BEHAVIOR. "To be good" is not an adequate target behavior. Narrow the disruptive student's behavior to *one* explicit, reasonable, and observable target behavior that you want lessened or increased. Usually the teacher, in causing an improvement in one stressful behavior, will find that other related behaviors are also improved. If, each day, a fifth-period class is lethargic, hyped up, or disruptive to the extent that they are off-task and nonproductive, the following precise, reasonable, and observable target behavior would be appropriate for a contingency management plan: "Each student will keep on-task between 2:00 p.m. and 2:50 p.m. each day. No student will be off-task longer than ten seconds." Teachers wishing to reduce talking in the room might adopt the following target behavior: "Before talking, each student must first raise a hand and be acknowledged by the teacher."

COLLECT AND GRAPH THE BASELINE DATA. Before initiating the contingency plan, but after determining the target behavior to be changed, either the teacher or an observer should run a frequency count for approximately five to seven days. Using the above target behavior requiring students to remain on task, a teacher's tally and graph might resemble figure 2.5.

The frequency count is meant to verify the intensity of the problem and the misbehaviors. Managers often are under such pressure that they incorrectly identify the severity and the cause of problems. For example, a teacher may believe one youngster to be the ringleader and the catalyst behind recurring problems but, upon analyzing the behavior of clique members, may find another

FIGURE 2.5 *Target behavior tally and graph.*

Monday:	⊞	⊞	⊞	II
Tuesday:	⊞	IIII		
Wednesday:	⊞	⊞	⊞	⊞	III
Thursday:	⊞	⊞	⊞	IIII
Friday:	⊞	⊞	⊞	⊞	II
Monday:	⊞	⊞	III	
Tuesday:	⊞	⊞	⊞	⊞

Now make a graph depicting your tallies.

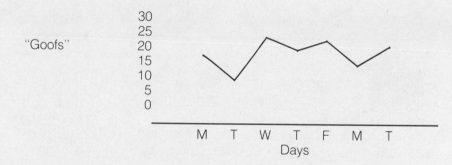

"Goofs"

to be the instigator. A third purpose is to have a basis for determining the relative success of the plan later. A graph prepared from the daily behaviors before the plan is implemented can later be compared with the number of behaviors that have occurred. This comparison serves as an evaluation of the manager's effectiveness and serves as a reinforcer: he or she can see the success.

DETERMINE THE TOKEN AND ITS ADMINISTRATIVE PROCEDURE. Since token secondary reinforcers are "tentative payment" for students accomplishing the target behavior, there must be a subsystem for redeeming the desired rewards. Anything less than a carefully planned token system will undermine the opportunity to successfully change students' behavior. The chosen token should be an item or act which is easily administered. The use of marbles as tokens would cause disturbances because they would be dropped and rolled, whereas issuing poker chips or marking a point card

FIGURE 2.6 *Point Card*

Student: _____

Date: _____

1	11	21	31	41
2	12	22	32	42
3	13	23	33	43
4	14	24	34	44
5	15	25	35	45
6	16	26	36	46
7	17	27	37	47
8	18	28	38	48
9	19	29	39	49
10	20	30	40	50

could eliminate that disturbing influence. Managers using poker chips or some other tangible token sometimes carry the items in a carpenter's apron.

The tokens should be issued immediately and consistently after the desired response. An example would be to issue one token at five-minute intervals to each student who is working consistently on the assignments.

Additional reinforcement principles include the following:

1. Do not insist on perfect performance on the first attempt. Start with relatively easy requirements.
2. Several days after the desired behavior is firmly established, lengthen the time and/or tasks.
3. Do not punish by taking away tokens earned earlier.
4. Ignore rule breakers as long as the rights and safety of other students are not violated.

Set times must be established for children to exchange their tokens for rewards. Teachers of primary-age children should establist at least one or two daily reward periods during which students may trade tokens for tangible rewards and activities. Older students require less frequent, but consistently adhered to, redemption periods.

DEVELOP AND POST THE MENU. The menu showing the rewards and their token values should be displayed along with the target behavior, assignments, and other announcements and directions. Since reinforcers are rewarding only when they are highly prized, it is incumbent on contingency managers to frequently add to and modify the menu.

FIGURE 2.7   *Example of Reinforcer Menu*

Reward	Cost	Time
Be leader of flag salute	5	one day
Receive ticket to high school basketball game	30	once
Be in magazine and comic book corner	10	15 minutes
Receive comic book	25	once
Observe filmstrip	10	10 minutes
Listen to records and recordings	10	10 minutes
Participate in spelling/math contest	10	once
Clean erasers	5	once
Carry message to office	5	once
Write letter	10	15 minutes
Work in science/math center	10	15 minutes
Be teacher assistant	5	once
Receive box of raisins	20	once
Go on extra trip to library	10	15 minutes
Have time in the overstuffed chair	10	10 minutes
Care for class pet	5	once

SOCIAL REINFORCERS WITH TOKENS. A contingency token plan should be implemented with the intent of phasing it out when the target behavior has reached a suitable frequency. The system's goal is to "help the child perform the target behavior not for a tangible reward but for the satisfaction of personal achievement" (Walker and Shea, 1984, p. 28). Because of contingency management's somewhat exorbitant time and administrative requirements, it is more costly than managing a classroom strictly by social reinforcers, body language, effective instructional techniques, and authoritative status. To make the transition from giving tokens for good behavior to giving unplanned social reinforcers, the issuance of tokens should always be accompanied by social rewards. Once the behavior is firmly established, the tangible tokens and rewards are given intermittently and are then gradually extinguished while maintaining the issuance of the social rewards for the target behavior. The contingency management plan sheet (figure 2.8) will serve to remind planners to consider not only this method for fading or extinguishing the tangible reinforcers, but also other minimal steps and methods required in designing a token management system.

Measures of Force Involved in the Contingency Management Model
Energy exerted in the following: Practicing the belief that it is better to catch children being good and then reward them. Thoroughly planning the management system Using consistency in administering the plan Collecting baseline data Determining the token, its value, and its administrative procedures Consistently employing social reinforcers Accumulating a list of desirable primary reinforcers

FIGURE 2.8

CONTINGENCY MANAGEMENT PLAN SHEET

Baseline Information:
Describe in observable terms the target behavior that is to be changed.

Daily record of the target behavior
Day	Times it occurred	What was your corrective behavior?
Monday		
Tuesday		
Wednesday		
Thursday		
Friday		

44

(continued)

Graph: Baseline data before plan

```
                        12
                        11
                        10
                         9
                         8
Times misbehaved,        7
or properly behaved      6
                         5
                         4
                         3
                         2
                         1
                         0
        _____

               M    T    W    T    F
```

Plan: Is the behavior described above to be lessened or increased?
       What token reinforcer is to be used?
       How often and how much of the token is to be given?
       What praise will accompany the issuance of the token?
Reinforcers: What is the menu and relative value of the token?
             When can the tokens be traded in and what is the proce-
             dure?
             What is the tentative plan for fading?

Graph: Behavior for first week of plan

```
                        12
                        11
                        10
                         9
                         8
Times misbehaved,        7
or properly behaved      6
                         5
                         4
                         3
                         2
                         1
                         0
        _____

               M    T    W    T    F
```

Evaluation:
       Has the target behavior improved? By what percentage?
       Are modifications required?

Canter's assertive behavior

Marlene and Lee Canter's (1976) Assertive Discipline system and the use of computers in the classroom are undoubtedly the two most popular pedagogic innovations of the 1980s. Each has been widely adopted: computers because of a blitz advertising campaign and a fear that the unexposed child will suffer in our futuristic, highly technological society, and assertive discipline because of easy implementation and great practicality. Assertive discipline is different from many other management models in that it provides a system for dealing with behavior at the time it occurs through a plan which makes the student responsible for his or her behavior and the resulting consequences.

Being an assertive teacher is very different from being an aggressive teacher. An aggressive person often bullies others with threats and loud speech. This type of teacher can be described as "one who lights up a room by leaving it." On the other hand, assertiveness is shown by a teacher making calm but firm declarations and calmly enforcing rules of conduct. Assertive teachers also consistently enforce rules and policies, make appropriate eye contact, face students when talking to them, and do not ask rhetorical questions when a specific behavior is required of a student ("Patti, will you stop looking out the window—O.K.?") Marlene and Lee Canter's assertive discipline formalizes these and other assertive behaviors into a plan of action for managing classrooms.

Assertive teachers do not threaten or express an intention to hurt. Instead, they give promises that are fulfilled each time a class rule is violated. When they inform a student that he or she will miss recess the next time the student is tardy, they unemotionally keep the student in during recess immediately following the next offense. Because students know the rules and consequences, they have the opportunity to choose good or poor conduct and to therefore choose to receive either an undesired or negative consequence, or a positive consequence. Managers who have planned well do not prepare their management system on the first day of classes. The plan, which should be thoroughly explained and initiated on the first day of school, is designed and made ready before school opens. It is especially important to determine a few behaviors and rules that will be consistently enforced, the unpleasant consequence for violators, the positive consequences for good behavior, and the process for administering the consequences, and then to communicate the plan's specifics to all involved persons.

Rules. The rules, which should not number more than four or five, are to be reasonable, observable, and enforceable. Some teachers prefer to keep conduct rules (no talking without permission) separate from academic rules (work independently on seatwork). Rules should be more specific than "be good" when, for example, you wish to regulate talking, but not too specific ("no talking"). A compromise would be to have the students "raise hands before speaking." Rules should be printed and posted so that they are legible from all points in the room. Since different activities may require different lists of rules and directions, it is wise to prepare, in advance, charts with different sets of rules and directions so that instructional time will not be unnecessarily used for this purpose when changing activities.

FIGURE 2.9

Charts for Rules and Consequences

CLASSROOM RULES	CONSEQUENCES (If you break a rule.)
1. _____	1st time: _____
2. _____	2nd time: _____
3. _____	3rd time: _____
4. _____	4th time: _____
5. _____	5th time: _____
	Severe disruption _____

Consequences. Marlene and Lee Canter (1976, p. 7) suggest that the consequences for violating rules be thoroughly explained and posted. The following serve as two examples of consequential plans or "menus."

FIGURE 2.10 *Example of consequence menus.*

Sequence of Violations	Consequence
First	= name on board (this is a warning)
Second	= one check by name (miss recess)
Third	= second check (isolate within classroom)
Fourth	= third check (call parent)
Fifth	= fourth check (out of room, that is, another classroom or to principal)

Sequence of Violations	Consequence
First	= name on board (warning)
Second	= one check (miss some specified privilege, for example, learning center)
Third	= second check (15 minutes after school, parents must be informed)
Fourth	= third check (30 minutes after school)
Fifth	= fourth check (send to principal)

Communications. Communications play an integral role in successfully administering assertive discipline. The discipline plan (management system) should be discussed with and receive the approval of the building principal, an important member of the teacher's disciplinary plan. The principal then knows that any child coming to his or her office from an assertive discipline classroom has misbehaved four previous times that day or has caused a severe disruption within the class. The teacher also knows what action the principal will consistently impose on violators. The principal who has been fully informed will know that once checkmarks are given they are not erased for good behavior, that the plan applies to all students, that all names and checks are erased at the end of each day, and that it may be necessary to make the plan stricter if it is not working after a few days.

Like the principal, parents are informed by letter of the teacher's management system. They are made aware of the teacher's attitude regarding the importance of good conduct and its influence on learning, of the class rules, of consequences, and of the school's desire to have the parents as partners in educating their children. Parents are particularly important when working with the "I don't care" child. These youngsters often create in the teacher a feeling of not knowing what to do next, which can increase the teacher's desire to retaliate with an equally defiant act. The Canters (1976, p. 109) recommend promising such a child that on the next offense the youngster's parents will be called. If the child repeats the behavior, he or she should be taken to the office and told to dial the parent's number at home or at work. The defiant student will probably change into a pleading one.

Beyond the third check. Consequences may be varied to increase the system's effectiveness and compatability with the teacher. For instance, the fourth consequence of sending students to the principal may be varied by sending the misbehaver to another teacher's classroom—one who earlier agreed to the plan. This colleague must be an effective disciplinarian. While in the colleague's classroom, the student will do prescribed work for thirty minutes, will not be allowed to participate in the receiving teacher's lessons and discussion, and will sit in the back of the room.

An in-school suspension room is a consequence used in some schools for working with severe behavior problems. The rooms, which are monitored by a certified person, require referred students to silently do assigned work for the remainder of the day, as well as the following day. Referred students lose their recesses, eat lunch in semi-isolated areas, are escorted to the bathroom, and earn one to three extra hours of isolation if they disrupt the in-school suspension room. Student contracts and exclusion from school are other consequences used with chronic and severely disruptive students.

Recognition of good behavior. Some children are so desirous of attention that they will violate social norms and classroom rules in order to gain recognition, even when knowing that they will be caught and that negative consequences will be forthcoming. These children, and all of their peers, should be taught by the teacher's methods "that they can get the attention they want and need by acting appropriately, rather than inappropriately" (Canter and Canter, 1976, p. 119).

If you wish to develop a more positive environment by more frequently administering positive consequences, first recall and make a list of the behaviors desired of your students. The list may include different types of desired behaviors: conduct behavior (no talking without permission), academic behavior (complete home-work before the next day), and affective behavior (thank those who assist you). Next to each required behavior, list several different verbal responses. gestures, privileges, and rewards that could be provided. This list should be taped to your desk and periodically reviewed in order to encourage your continuing use of positive consequences.

The recipient of positive consequences may be an individual, a small group, or an entire class. The Canters (1976, pp. 140-141) state that teachers at all levels find the "marbles in a jar" conse-quence to be effective in encouraging appropriate behavior. This consequence requires only a jar and a bag of marbles. The marbles are dropped periodically when the entire class is working on the assigned task and behaving as directed. The sound made by the dropped marbles striking other marbles signals to all class mem-bers that the teacher is pleased with their behavior and that they have earned another minute of special activity time at the end of that day or some other designated time or day. Teachers must remain aware that the effectiveness of positive consequences is largely dependent on how much the potential recipient values the reward as well as the sincerity accompanying the reward.

Measures of Force Involved in Canters' Assertive Behavior
Energy exerted in the following: Learning to make calm but firm declarations   Learning to calmly and consistently enforce rules of conduct   Learning to refrain from asking rhetorical questions about misbe-havior   Replacing the issuance of threats with that of promises   Thoroughly explaining the system to students and posting the rules and consequences   Communicating the plan to the principal and parents   Developing a system for rewarding good behavior

Jones's management training

Some teacher-training institutions do little more than provide their trainees with a few vague management guidelines ("Be child centered") and a few trite and often misleading pearls of wisdom such as "Don't smile until Christmas." Frederic H. Jones believes that this lack of training continues to lessen the effectiveness of even the best teachers: "After years on the job, even the best teachers still function at a level far below that which could be achieved with focused training in management of discipline problems" (Jones, 1979, p. 27).

Jones's classroom management training program (CMTP) acknowledges that there is no single best method of dealing with discipline in the classroom. Rather, there are many different methods for different children in different circumstances and, as most educators will agree, every method of reducing classroom disruption and increasing productive work can fail or can be abused if done improperly.

As mentioned in chapter 1, Jones's research found that 80 percent of all classroom disruptions were nothing more than students talking to their neighbors and that most of the remaining disturbances were caused by students wandering about the room: that is, most classroom discipline problems were caused by "talking and walking." Such misbehaviors are minor infractions until their frequency compounds them into a major force which significantly impedes the teacher's instructional efforts.

Classrooms which are found to be loud and disorderly average as many as 2.5 disruptions per child per minute. In contrast, a well-managed room has a rate of approximately 0.6 disruptions per child per minute (Jones, 1979, p. 27). When disruptions occur, students become off task and achieve less. Therefore, if teachers have not learned and developed effective management techniques, their preparation and planning will probably result in wasted instructional time as well as additional teacher stress, lower supervisory evaluations, and a higher likelihood of becoming teacher dropout candidates.

Three of Jones's major procedures for managing student behavior are setting limits, using an incentive system, and giving assistance. The first, setting limits, is the act of consistently disallowing infractions of basic classroom rules (Jones, 1979, p. 28). Most classroom management systems are deficient in providing techniques for immediately suppressing behavior—with a minimal loss of instructional time. Jones's program is an exception, as is illustrated in the limit-setting steps that follow.

51

Jones's Limit Setting

1. Make a few rules which you will quickly and consistently enforce.

2. Respond immediately to violators. By not responding or slowly responding, you will be read as "I'll let you goof off as long as you don't get so unruly as to anger me or embarrass me" (Jones, 1979, p. 29).
   - Face the child squarely.
   - Say the child's name in a firm tone.
   - Look the child in the eye.

3. If child does not conform:
   - Move toward the child until your leg touches the edge of the desk.
   - Look the child in the eyes. When two children are involved, position yourself between them and look into the eyes of one student.
   - Keep your mouth shut. "You are now using body language that says you mean business" (Jones, 1979, p. 29).

   If the child still does not turn around, sit up, or return to work:
   - Put the palms of your hands on the desk and move your shoulders and eyes down to his or her eye level.
   - If the child still does not correct the behavior, pause a moment, put your elbow on the desk, lean forward, and get eyeball to eyeball. When two children are involved, position yourself and orient yourself to one student by looking into his or her eyes.
   - Only say "Sit up," "Turn around," or "Get to work."

   If the child says, "I wasn't doing anything" or "I was just answering her question" or "Get away from me":
   - Move an inch closer to the child's face, keep your cool, and don't get verbally engaged.
   - When the child runs out of excuses, say firmly, "Sit up," "Turn around," or "Get to work."
   - When the child "caves in" and complies, become warm and nurturant and say "thank you."
   - Then stand up and pull away slowly, retaining eye contact.

The body language directed above is all important in bringing about students' compliance. It is the body language of an interaction between two people that communicates the participant's firmness of conviction and emotional state. An effective classroom manager's body language usually communicates a state of being unemotional, consistent, firm, a person of few words, and softly spoken when enforcing rules.

When the above steps become ineffective with a student, the child should be placed in an isolated area (see chapter 7). This step will convince most students that the teacher is serious about enforcing class rules. The chronic disrupter may force the teacher to cease using isolation when it takes too much time from the instructional program. In these few instances, an incentive system as described below for secondary students may be more appropriate.

Secondary students are less appropriate clients for Jones's limit-setting techniques. High school students are frequently very protective of their self-concepts and often will not tolerate an invasion of their life space by the teacher placing an elbow on their desk and getting physically close. Therefore, it is better to use Jones's limit setting with only those secondary students who are not likely to physically retaliate. For others, consider using an incentive system. Indeed, there are situations in which limit setting is not the best approach, and in most situations it should be used in conjunction with a class incentive system.

Trainees who feel that this approach is too obtrusive for their personalities should realize that the act of getting "eyeball to eyeball" will be necessary only during early confrontations, and then only periodically thereafter when students are learning and relearning that the teacher means business. Most will learn very early that disruptive behavior is not worth having a confrontation with the teacher. Later on children's behavior is corrected by less intimidating desist techniques: eye contact, calling the child's name, or making a hand gesture.

Jones's incentive system. Jones reminds his trainees that incentive systems are based on Grandma's rule, "You must finish your dinner before you get your dessert," and that an incentive system has three primary parts: a task, a reward, and a procedure for strict accountability (Jones, 1979, p. 30). The task must be

53

reasonable as to the child's and school's values, at a consonant level in being harmonious with his abilities to achieve the task, and observable. The *rewards* which must be highly desired by the students, may be reinforcers such as tokens, stickers, trinkets, or preferred activities. The system's designer must initially identify numerous reinforcers that can be rotated before satiation. The *accountability* procedure identifies when and how the reinforcers will be consistently administered.

Jones's program recognizes the inappropriateness of the limit-setting method when the teacher is attempting to keep two-thirds of the class doing independent seatwork while working with the other third in a reading circle. The steps of limit setting are unsuitable in such a situation because the teacher cannot remain instructionally effective with the reading circle if he or she must leave to become physically close to a seatwork disturber. In such cases an incentive approach as outlined below with slight modifications to Jones's teachings will prove more appropriate than the limit-setting method.

1. Obtain a stopwatch with two buttons so that the elapsed time can be recorded.

2. Together with the students, determine a preferred activity of fifteen minutes duration.

3. Announce the following instructions:

    > I will meet with each reading group for fifteen minutes; therefore our reading class will go on for approximately fifty minutes.

    > Notice this stopwatch. When we have done forty minutes of good work, we will have a preferred activity period.

    > If anyone violates our class rules, I will call his or her name and stop the watch until you correct your behavior and return to your assigned task.

    > This means that for every minute that the watch is stopped, you will all lose one minute of preferred activity time.

Take a look at the posted class rules and the assignment written on the chalkboard. Are there any questions?

Group 1 report to the reading circle with your readers. Group 2 and group 3 start your seatwork assignments. I'm pushing the clock's start button—so let's go!

4. The teacher must frequently scan the seatworkers while at the same time instructing the circle's participants.

5. When a seatworker or circle participant breaks a rule, the teacher states the student's name, holds up the stopwatch in an obvious manner, and presses the stop button—hopefully with an audible click.

6. If the child does not immediately return to work, the teacher stares at the child until he or she returns to the assigned task—even when the child offers excuses. The misbehaver's peers will often pressure him or her to return to work so that their own preferred activity time is not lost.

Jones maintains that the incentive approach described above can be used effectively with different instructional groupings and with primary-age children up through the secondary grades. Teachers of secondary students usually provide only one preferred activity period per week, whereas teachers of primary children will necessarily employ several preferred activity periods per day. Recalling Jones's earlier acknowledgment that no one management procedure is appropriate for all students at all times, one should remember that some children may require a different management system other than limit setting and the incentive approach.

Instructional methods. Jones recognizes instructional methods as a third major aspect of effective classroom management. Good instructional skills and methods produce greater student achievement and reduce the number of classroom disturbances by uninterested and lower-achieving students. One instructional skill of profound importance in that of assisting learners.

Teachers usually invest most of each study period with students in need of help—often averaging four minutes per student visit (Jones, 1979, p. 31). These time investments allow helping sessions for only seven students during a thirty-minute study period—leaving all others to work without words of encouragement and prompting about how to continue solving and achieving. When two-thirds of the students—some helplessly stuck and others desirous of "teacher strokes"—are forced to work without teacher contact, then unproductive behavior is likely to ensue. To remedy this situation, the teacher needs to reduce the visit's duration and to increase the number of assists. At twenty seconds per visit the teacher can provide up to ninety assists in a thirty-minute study period. A more detailed explanation of Jones's assisting procedure, sometimes called "Praise, Prompt, and Leave," is presented in chapter 6 under the topic of seatwork assistance.

Measures of Force Involved in Jones's Management Training

Energy exerted in the following:
Making rules which will be quickly enforced
Consistently disallowing infractions of rules
Learning and implementing Jones's body language and procedures for stopping misbehavior
Remaining unemotional and firm in correcting behavior
Developing an incentive system
Implementing the "stopwatch approach" when working with one group for an extended period
Implementing the "Praise, Prompt, and Leave" approach

Questions and tasks

Counseling

1. What is the difference between direct and nondirect counseling?

2. Does a nondirect counselor feed children's feelings back to them in order to verify their statement? Explain.

3. What are four characteristics of a nondirect counselor?

4. If nondirect counselors are absolutely certain that their suggestion would solve the student's problem, is it alright to make the recommendation? Explain.

5. Whom do students and adults seek as their counselors?

6. Be able to provide the correct dialogue if asked to use nondirect counseling.

7. Why does a direct counselor not start a conference by asking why the student behaved as he or she did?

8. Why does the counselor express sympathy for the feelings of a student who has misbehaved?

9. Why should the counselor preface his or her suggestions?

Ginott's congruent communication

1. What is the meaning of "congruent communications" as advocated by Ginott?

2. How does Ginott feel about punishment? Why?

3. A teacher at his or her best corrects students by doing what?

4. A teacher at his or her worst handles misbehaviors by doing what?

5. Why are "I" messages better than "you" messages when dealing with misbehavior?

6. What links Ginott's system with Gordon's teacher effectiveness training and Roger's client-centered therapy?

7. What is Charles's comment about the incompleteness of Ginott's model as a complete management system?

Maslow's hierarchy of needs

1. Although incomplete as a management model, Maslow's hierarchy has an important message for classroom managers. What is the message?

2. When, according to Maslow's hierarchy, do discipline problems develop?

3. Be able to list and discuss man's needs in correct sequence.

4. What is a complaint against the logic of Maslow's hierarchy?

5. According to Maslow's model, what is a possible reason for a shy and unpopular child not learning?

Values and morality

1. In what way do the teachings of Raths and Kohlberg agree?

2. According to Raths, discipline problems result from one of two conditions. What are they?

3. Do some adults profess values that are not a part of their conscience?

4. Think of an instance in which a conflict developed because two people possessed different values.

5. Kohlberg believes that advanced stages of morality are dependent on a person's ability to reason abstractly. Do you agree? Why?

6. Explain Kohlberg's six stages of moral reasoning by outlining the key traits and examples of each.

7. Is it wrong for teachers to teach values and morality? Explain your answer.

8. Give two examples in which conflicts may develop if the teacher does not recognize a student's level of moral development.

9. What is meant by the expression that "if values are not taught, they are caught"?

Transactional analysis

1. What is the logic behind the statement that "a dialogue between two individuals may result in nine combinations of ego states?"

2. Explain each of the three ego states with no more than five words each.

3. As directed in the text, identify each statement on page 28 as being in the child, parent, or adult state.

4. Teachers should remain in which ego state? Why?

Dreikurs's mistaken goal model

1. Does Dreikurs recommend allowing young students to help establish rules? Explain.

2. Name and explain the model's two types of consequences.

3. Dreikurs believes that consequences are best predetermined. Why?

4. The teacher should not be used as a punisher but as an enforcer. What is the difference?

5. Who *finally* chooses the consequence for misbehavior?

6. What do we want the student to develop? What will help him or her to develop that thing?

7. Charles notes that the system has three underlying beliefs. What are they?

8. This system is largely based on the belief that discipline problems are largely caused by students wanting acceptance, recognition, and attention. Why is the model called "mistaken goal"?

9. List the four "mistaken goals" followed by two probing questions that may get the student to examine why he or she is exhibiting the undesirable behavior.

Glasser's reality therapy

1. How does Glasser's system disregard the concerns of psychoanalysts and educators?

2. Do you agree with Glasser that students are responsible for their behavior and the resulting consequences?

3. Do you agree that teachers should not accept excuses for poor behavior? Explain.

4. What does Glasser say about rules?

5. How are Glasser's views about consequences similar to those of Dreikurs?

6. Be able to list and explain each of Glasser's ten steps.

7. Why does Glasser say that step 3 is the most important?

8. Which step is omitted for secondary students? Why?

9. What does Glasser say about punishment?

10. Practice using the appropriate dialogue for steps 4, 5, and 6.

11. Glasser qualifies his plan. How?

12. Charles points out one drawback to Glasser's system. What is Charles's concern?

Contingency management

1. What is the difference between primary and secondary reinforcers? Give two examples of each not provided in the text.

2. How is contingency management more of a "catching children being good" approach than most traditional management systems?

3. Why are users of contingency management asked to ignore misbehavior?

4. What are the characteristics of a good target behavior? List two target behaviors not presented in the text.

5. Listed are four types of reinforcers. List two examples of each that were not presented in the text.
    Social:
    Token:
    Activity:
    Tangible:

6. Be able to describe a contingency system in which the primary reinforcer is immediately provided after the correct response.

7. What are three problems to guard against when immediately providing the reward?

8. Think of a hypothetical target behavior and then complete the contingency management plan sheet in accordance with the previously described procedures.

9. Why is "to be good" not a good target behavior?

10. Why is it that usually when one misbehavior is corrected that other misbehaviors also seem to improve?

11. Why is the gathering of baseline data important initially and later after the plan has been initiated?

12. Why should the manager not insist on perfect performance on the first attempt after implementing the plan?

13. How do you feel about not taking away earlier earned tokens for misbehavior?

14. What do you think would be appropriate times during the week to have reward periods in grade two, grade seven, and grade ten?

15. What would be a good method for determining a list of highly prized rewards?

16. What is the purpose of giving rewards?

17. When should social reinforcers be administered?

Canter's assertive behavior

1. What are some characteristics of an "assertive" teacher? What is the difference between assertive and aggressive?

2. Does the assertive discipline play really provide students with a choice of consequences? Explain.

3. Do you think that conduct rules and academic rules should be mixed or kept separate? Why?

4. Develop a set of four conduct rules for your future classroom.

5. Develop a menu of consequences for breaking the above rules.

6. Why is a "severe clause" included and explained to the students?

7. Who else, besides the teacher, should know about the assertive discipline plan? In each case, why?

8. How could a "strong" colleague help with children who go "beyond the third check"?

9. What is the advantage of taping a list of social reinforcers to your desk?

10. Explain how to use the "marbles in a jar" procedure.

Jones's management training

1. Do Jones's 80 percent findings seem reasonable or unreasonable? Why?

2. If a secondary school's instructional day is 290 minutes long and each class averages twenty-five students, how many estimated disruptions in a day will a teacher experience if the classroom is loud and disorderly?
   How many for the teacher in a well-managed classroom?
   If student achievement is positively correlated with time on task, what should be the salary of the teacher with a loud and disorderly classroom if pay were based on effectiveness?

3. Summarize Jones's three major procedures for managing student behavior.
   Limit setting:
   Incentive system:
   Giving assistance:

4. Be able to fully explain Jones's limit-setting procedure.

5. What is body language?
   If you became a substitute teacher tomorrow, what body language would you want to communicate to the students?

6. Why is Jones's limit-setting technique less appropriate for secondary students?

7. How frequently does an effective teacher get "eyeball to eyeball" with a student? Why?

8. What is a drawback to the limit-setting method?

9. Be able to thoroughly explain Jones's stopwatch incentive approach.

10. In many classrooms, students spend a larger amoung of time doing seatwork than they spend listening to and working directly with the teacher. Is this the way it should be? Explain your answer.

11. What is Jones's recommendation for helping students with their seatwork?

Part II

The Relationship of Research to Classroom Management

3

Research Relating to the Improvement of Instruction and Classroom Management

"American education is on the mend; we still have a long way to go." Those were the words of William J. Bennett, secretary of education, when asked by the media to react to the 1985 Scholastic Aptitude Test (SAT) scores, which showed the biggest increase since 1963. These gains, plus a slight increase in the American College Test (ACT) scores, have been hailed by some educators as proof that reform is taking hold in the public schools of our nation.

Indeed, there does appear to be an awakening on the part of governors, legislators, and educators, an awareness that leaders can improve education by recognizing and requiring programs that are congruent with the findings of educational researchers. Many of these findings became available to the nation's citizenry and legislators through the reports of several groups which undertook the task of studying our nation's public schools and then made recommendations for change. The most frequently quoted study commission of the 1980s was the National Commission on Excellence in Education, whose 1983 report, *A Nation at Risk: The Imperatives for Educational Reform,* produced a shock intense enough to cause legislators and governors across this nation to pass legislation and necessary funding for educational reform.

As educators, we can take little credit for the reform movement, as minor as it is, because the "effectiveness research" which was the basis for the recommendations coming out of different educational study groups had been available to educators for several years but was largely ignored. We have made little use of educational research in the practices of our nation's schools. The study commissions have indeed caused a needed ripple effect among legislators and educators. It is to be hoped that the change will not prove to be short-lived, that some educators will not continue to expend minimal effort even when their professional behavior contradicts the findings of educational researchers. Berliner (1984, p. 74) asks, "What will it take to convince the teacher education community to use such knowledge?" Regardless of the amount and durability of the changes recommended by the reports of various commissions, an equal or more important outcome may be the way legislators and the public critique us in our professional roles. Now that the legislators and public have forced change upon us, we may become more sensitive and prone to act on our own knowledge about teaching effectiveness.

Only the unlearned educator would doubt the existence of educational research that has practical value for increasing student achievement, teacher effectiveness, and the managerial competencies of teachers. But are research-proven procedures also important for those instructors who have not been formally trained in pedagogy but are successful teachers? Such individuals are undoubtedly perceptive in discovering essential instructional techniques and possess the necessary human relations skills required to be adequate instructors or even outstanding ones. It is not to be supposed that each successful teacher is a product of formal pedagogical training any more than that every successful lawyer has been a recipient of college degrees and certificates. There is an art, as well as a science, to practicing both professions. But the art portion, the natural aptitude, is not entirely unlearned or instinctive. "Natural teachers" have learned by reflecting on their own experiences as learners and by trial-and-error experiences on the job: Qui docet discit—"He who teaches, learns." Teachers who are products of up-to-date training institutions possess both a degree of natural aptitude and knowledge of pedagogical foundations, theories, skills, and methods. This knowledge provides them with a fuller repertoire of approaches for dealing with a multitude of situations arising from dealing with twenty to fifty pupils—children with different backgrounds, needs, and abilities. But the trainees' repertoire will not be appropriately filled if their training institutions do not infuse current knowledge and research findings into the required curriculum. Personnel at *all* levels of our profession must continue to learn, share, and implement research-proven practices if teaching is ever to be universally accepted as a profession. *Professionals* do not ignore the teachings of their profession.

Today's training institutions are blessed with an increasing knowledge base for both preservicing trainees and inservicing practicing teachers.

> From this body of literature [research findings] we can begin for the first time to distill some empirically validated principles to guide future classroom organizational, management, and instructional efforts. These findings provide an empirical base for building an entire classroom system for success (Paine et al. 1983, p. 15).

Paine's belief that institutions can train educators by providing them with research-validated principles and procedures has been supported by success stories from many of the nation's school systems. In one study, in which the treatment teachers received six workshops which were based on findings from research on time allocation and interactions, their students gained, on the average, six months more in reading advancement than did the control teachers' students. A late-spring observation indicated that treatment teachers maintained most of their behavior changes, whereas control teachers' classes became more lax and less task oriented. The findings of renowned researchers such as Good and Grouws fortify Paine's beliefs: they found that teachers inserviced in instructional methods "performed more of the treatment behavior than did the control teachers" and that "the performance of the treatment group exceeds the performance of the control group" (1979, pp. 355-362).

School districts such as the Charlotte-Mecklenburg district are attempting to upgrade instruction by supervising, inservicing, and evaluating new teachers on *competencies* (knowledge and skills) assumed to be necessary to meet *expectations* that the system holds for experienced teachers (Schlechty, 1985). The Charlotte-Mecklenburg district feels that teachers can be fairly evaluated only if they are knowledgeable about the professional literature associated with effective teaching. The Charlotte teachers are observed and rated in five classroom performance areas: management of instructional time, management of student behavior, instructional presentations, monitoring, and feedback. It is interesting to note that these evaluative criteria, which are strongly emphasized throughout this book and which are supported by research, are radically different from those held by districts that evaluate teachers on unsupported personality traits.

It is important to know about and implement instructional and management research findings not only to enhance academic achievement but also to improve classroom management practices. Usually, the techniques that bring about higher achievement are directly related to effective classroom management. We can accurately state that good instruction usually prevents discipline problems and, in turn, that good classroom management provides an environment conducive to academic achievement. Susan Rosenholtz (1985) sums up the relationship of discipline to effective teaching as follows: "Teachers who must focus their energies on controlling disruptive students do so at the expense of instructional time and of their own instructional improvement" (p. 351).

Below are some *samples* of research findings on the characteristics of effective teachers—teachers whose students learn more, and who have well-managed classrooms. The findings were randomly selected and categorized into groups only for the purpose of alerting trainees to the existence of validated principles that can be used in guiding their instructional and management practices. However, David Berliner warns us that we should not make the mistake of believing that any one of the following factors alone will significantly increase achievement and attentiveness (though it may): "Instructional behavior is multifaceted and it is, no doubt, the interaction of dozens of significant variables like these that affect achievement" (Berliner, 1984, p. 65). Because each of the following research findings has a practical message for teachers, trainees should conceptualize and synthesize each of them into their own developing, personalized management system. The chapter which follows this one will discuss how the findings on one subject—time on task—have been used to improve instruction.

Research summaries

Expectations, attitudes, and emphasis

Brophy and Evertson (1976) found that teachers who were getting the most achievement from students were those who perceived students as capable of learning schoolwork and who viewed themselves as capable of teaching the curriculum.

Teachers' expectations contribute significantly to student levels of achievement and classroom behavior (Brophy and Evertson, 1976; Good and Brophy, 1978). For example, Good and Brophy found that teachers tended to seat low-performing students further away from themselves, called on those students less, and praised them fewer times.

Teacher emphasis on academic goals is positively associated with student learning. Such teachers are not "cold" but emphasize the importance of school learning (Fisher et al., 1981).

Some teachers in one study placed primary emphasis on affective outcomes—music, personal development, and good feelings. Under these conditions, both academic learning time (ALT) and achievement were relatively low (Fisher et al., 1981).

"It has been found that the teachers in high-achievement schools appear to be distinguished from those in less effective schools by the belief that students can and will learn. Teachers in these high-achievement schools also seem to be more active classroom teachers" (Brookover et al., 1978).

Rutter and others (1979) have found marked differences in outcomes of secondary schools that were attributable to school-level variables such as expectations. If teachers set high but attainable goals for academic performance, academic achievement usually increases.

Ornstein (1981) has noted that Medley examined 289 studies and concluded that the effective teacher directly emphasizes academic activities and devotes more class time to academic skills than does the ineffective teacher.

The relationship between teachers' characteristics and student learning has typically been represented by correlations of less than

+.20. (Characteristics: attitude, sex, age, training, personality, and membership in organizations.) Soar et al. speak unfavorably about the validity of supervisors using such characteristics by saying "no faith can be placed in the findings of such studies (1983, p. 240). These researchers believe a better way "lies in the use of low-inference measures of teacher performance that have been developed through research on teacher-effectiveness. (p. 246).

Consequences

Frequent reprimands are negatively associated with student learning. When students are sometimes unable to do tasks, they do not work. The need for frequent reminders and reprimands may be a signal for reteaching or employing a different prescription (Fisher et al., 1981).

Loss of privileges has been shown to be a powerful intervention when used in combinations with praise and other reinforcers (Walker, Hops, and Fieginbaum, 1976).

Forehand et al. (1976) showed that when negative attention (verbal reprimands), time-out, and ignoring were compared, each procedure was effective in modifying noncompliance; however, the negative attention procedure was associated with increased on-task behavior.

High-achieving classes tend to have some type of positive reward system (Fisher et al., 1981).

Teacher criticism of student behavior, shouting, scolding, ridicule, and sarcasm have a consistently negative relation to achievement gain (Solomon and Kendall, 1976).

Research has shown that praising one student can influence other children nearby (Broden et al., 1970; Kazdin, 1973).

O'Leary et al. (1970) have demonstrated that a teacher's loud reprimands actually increase the disruptive behavior of an entire class, while soft reprimands reduce them. Interestingly, the quiet reprimand has a similar effect as praising, that is, appropriate behavior increases when the procedure is implemented.

Clarity and firmness help induce orderly behavior; roughness seems to produce anxiety and disruptive behavior (Gordon and Jester, 1973).

Kash and Borich (1978) have summarized the current research on praise. They generalize that teacher praise is positively correlated with academic achievement for students of low socioeconomic status but has either no relationship or a negative correlation with achievement for students of higher socioeconomic status.

Rohrkemper and Brophy (1980) have noted that effective managers "punish less, were more supportive and reassuring . . . and were more likely to use contracts, thus involving the student in his/her own behavior change."

Kounin and Gump (1961) have found that children who have excessively punitive teachers manifest more aggression in their misconduct.

Lasley (1981) have found that public corrections often cause students to lose face and force students to retaliate or become aggressive. Private, individualized corrections enable the teacher and the misbehaving student to work problems out without fearing what others may think if either "backs down."

Instructional methods

Time spent working with textbooks, as opposed to time spent with puzzles, games, and toys, is related to achievement in reading and math (Stallings, 1980).

Fisher and others (1980) have concluded that students pay more attention when the teachers spend time communicating the goals of the lesson and giving directions. The lesson needs to be structured so that students know why the lesson is occurring. Naturally, structuring should not be overdone to the degree that the directions are excessive and boring.

Children in kindergarten through third grade tend to respond best to direct instruction, small steps of progress, a rapid pace, over-teaching of content (overlearning), and teacher praise (Brophy and Evertson, 1976).

Stallings has reported that teachers have better results if they clearly state the activity's educational objectives. The more the students know about the purpose of a lesson, the greater the interest level and ability to retain the material. Teachers should also state their expectations about the quality of work (AASA, 1982).

71

Brophy has observed that direct instruction may be needed most by anxious pupils who exhibit low ability or achievement motivation (McFaul, 1983).

Peterson's review of studies suggests that "high achieving, task oriented students do worse in direct instruction than in less direct approaches," whereas less able students perform better in teacher-directed, large-group situations (McFaul, 1983).

Anderson, Evertson, and Brophy (1979) have stressed the importance of overteaching and making sure that each student "is checked, receives feedback, and achieves mastery."

Preventing classroom management problems by planning and preparing is the most effective way to provide a suitable environment for individual and group learning (Brophy and Putman, 1978).

"The basic concept emerging from recent process-product findings is active teaching. A teacher sets and articulates learning goals, actively assesses student progress, and frequently makes class presentations illustrating how to do assigned work. Active teaching does not occur when teachers do not actively present the process of concept under study, when they fail to supervise student seatwork actively, or if they do not hold students accountable for their work" (Good, 1982).

Monitoring

Research suggests that, when monitoring during seatwork, teacher contact with a student should be relatively short, averaging thirty seconds or less (Evertson, Emmer, and Brophy, 1980).

Emmer and Evertson have found that more successful managers monitor student behavior extensively and quickly attend to inappropriate behavior (Doyle, 1980).

The less effective teachers' poorer monitoring is caused by a variety of factors. Some simply do not circulate among students during seatwork and thereby diminish their ability to observe accurately. Other teachers work with only a few students during seatwork (Gump, 1969).

Seatwork

In different studies, examining hundreds of classrooms for students age eight to eleven, researchers found that students work privately about 50 percent of the time on ditto sheets, workbooks, etc. (Angus, Evans, and Parkin, 1975; McDonald, 1976).

Mason and Osburn have found that students spend as much time or more time with their workbooks as they do with their teachers (Eaton, 1984).

Students in grades one through seven spend more time working alone at seatwork than at any other activity (Evertson et al., 1980; Fisher et al., 1980). They are less engaged during seatwork than when they are in groups receiving instruction from the teacher.

In one study, successful teachers had the students work as a group on the first few seatwork problems before releasing them for seatwork (Anderson, Evertson, and Brophy, 1979).

Teachers who are successful managers of seatwork are actively circulating, asking questions, and giving explanations during seatwork. Fisher and others (1980) have found that when students have contact with the teacher (or another adult) during seatwork their engagement rate increases by 10 percent.

Investigators have not found any evidence that students are less satisfied when the sheer quantity of work is relatively great (Fisher et al., 1978).

Time allocations

The most general finding is that academic learning time is the most important variable influencing student learning (Ornstein and Levine, 1983).

Stallings (1975) has reported that low-achieving third grades in Follow Through prospered more from an increase in time spent in reading and math than did the higher-achieving students. Caution: For all students, there is a point at which more time does not produce more learning. Such curvilinear effects have been reported by Soar (1978).

Findings (Stallings, 1975; Stallings et al., 1979) indicate that increased length of class periods in secondary schools is not related to student academic achievement. Clearly, student learning depends on how the available time is used, not just the amount of time.

Fisher and others (1981) have found that the amount of time that teachers allocate to instructions in a particular curriculum content area is positively associated with student learning in that area. The study found that fifth grade reading varied from 60 to 140 minutes per day.

The proportion of allocated time that students are *engaged* is positively associated with learning. Two classes may allocate the same amount of time, but one class may have an engagement rate of 50 percent and another of 90 percent (Fisher et al., 1981).

The proportion of time that reading or mathematics tasks are performed with high success is positively associated with student learning (Fisher et al., 1981).

Students who spend more time than the average in highly successful activities have higher achievement scores in the spring, better retention over the summer, and more positive attitudes toward school (Fisher et al., 1981).

Managerial concerns

Kounin (1977) has found that successful classroom managers (1) deal with several things at once; (2) exhibit an ongoing awareness of all that is happening in the classroom despite numerous distractions; (3) do not get overly involved with one student at the expense of others; and (4) manage movement within the classroom by controlling student transitions.

Emmer, Evertson, and Anderson (1979) have reported that effective teachers (1) monitor students frequently; (2) intervene quickly to deal with behavior problems; (3) ensure high levels of time-on-task; (4) provide frequent and detailed feedback; (5) structure activities and materials carefully; (6) use task-signaling systems; and (7) establish clear routines and expectations and rehearse with students the behaviors that match those expectations.

Lasley (1981) has found that group commands are easy for misbehaving students to ignore.

"Teachers' managerial abilities have been found to relate positively to student achievement in every process-product study conducted to date" (Good, 1982).

"The effective teachers were better managers primarily because of their clear goals, commitment to teach these goals, and their systematic follow through" (Good, 1982).

Moskowitz and Hayman (1976) have found that discipline problems are often evoked in new teachers' classes by routine tasks, seatwork, and working individually with one student at a time; that new teachers structure fewer activities per class; and that they structure sedentary activities which often lead to student restlessness.

New teachers most frequently meet control problems by ignoring them and continuing to teach or by waiting until the situation is out of hand before trying to get order. They then resort to yelling, shouting, and whistling (Moskowitz and Hayman, 1976).

Accountability

Students are more likely to complete tasks when they know they will be held accountable (Fisher et al., 1981).

Good classroom managers keep track of whether students are completing assignments and staying on task (Emmer and Evertson, 1980). They check homework frequently and return graded papers, and they keep track of how students are progressing and completing assignments.

Location factor

Rist (1970) has found that teachers assign seating locations to students on variables other than the need for frequent monitoring.

Van Houten and others (1982) have found that physical proximity to the student being reprimanded is as important as eye contact.

Weinstein (1979) states that "it would seem that physical environment of the conventional classroom has little impact on achievement." When classrooms varying in terms of furniture arrangement, aesthetic appeal, and the presence or absence of windows are compared, differences in achievement are nonsignificant. The only physical variable that has been linked to differences in school achievement is seating location.

Schwebel and Cherlin (1972) have found research demonstrating that students near the front of the room are more attentive and more engaged in on-task behavior.

Adams and Biddle (1970) have found that a student's seating position can greatly affect the amount of interaction the student has with the teacher. Most of the teacher's interaction is with students who are seated in the center front portion of the class or in a line from the center front to the back of the room.

Krontz and Risley (1972) have experimentally demonstrated that spacing preschool disadvantaged children apart, rather than letting them crowd together, increases their attention to the teacher.

Rules

Stallings has found that when teachers and the principal have jointly developed a discipline policy that is clearly stated and consistently adhered to, student discipline problems decrease (ASCD, 1984).

Smith and Smith have found that effective rules meet certain criteria: (1) rules must be stated or taught so that those affected understand how they should behave; (2) rules must be reasonable and necessary; and (3) rules must be enforceable (Lasley, 1981).

Carolyn Evertson's study has indicated that teachers who spend the first week reminding the students of rules and reinforcing the penalties have fewer discipline problems as the year goes on (ASCD, 1984).

Emmer and Evertson (1980) have found that effective classroom managers have clearly defined rules and procedures (regarding call outs, movement, talk among students, hand raising, etc.). Some teachers do not have rules and some have rules but do not communicate consequences to the students. Other teachers have rules or procedures but do not always present them clearly or enforce them.

Testing and grading

Some educational reformers of the 1960s condemned grades, but the evidence is persuasive that grades do motivate students to learn more in a given subject (Gage and Berliner, 1984). Other studies show the importance of holding students accountable.

Do tests measure the curriculum? Freeman and others (1980) examined the topics in three widely used mathematics textbooks and each test item in five widely used standardized tests. In the *best* case, 29 percent of what was tested had never been covered in school by students. In the *worst* case, 47 percent of the topics that were tested had never been covered by the text.

The Van Houtens' 1977 study revealed the importance of publicly posting students' scores. This technique has also been effective in improving the academic performance of secondary students (Van Houten and Lai Fatt, 1981).

Feedback

Kulik and Kulik (1979) have found that instruction is more effective when (1) students receive immediate feedback on their examinations, and (2) students have to do further study and take another text when their quiz scores do not reach a criterion.

The percentage of instructional time during which the student receives feedback (answering questions, checking papers, using programmed texts, etc.) is positively related to student engagement rate and to achievement (Fisher et al., 1978).

Academic feedback (letting students know whether their answers are right or wrong, or giving them the right answer) is more strongly and consistently related to achievement than any other teaching behavior (Fisher et al., 1978).

Corrective feedback, contingent praise for correct behavior, and the use of students' ideas as a way of letting students know that their contributions are valued all show positive relations to achievement and attitude (Gage and Berliner, 1984). This feedback is not often found at high rates, despite its established effectiveness.

Time on task

The Beginning Teacher Evaluation Study (Fisher et al., 1978) has found an incredible variation in the time allocations made by different teachers. One fifth-grade teacher had 68 minutes of reading and the other had 137. A second-grade teacher allocated 47 minutes for reading and language arts, and another had 118 minutes a day.

One district that audited how time was spent in their schools added the equivalent of ten to sixteen days of instructional time per school year without lengthening the school day or year. That time, in that district, would have been worth 2 to 3 million dollars if it had to be purchased (Fisher et al., 1978).

If fifty minutes of reading instruction per day is allocated to a student who pays attention about one-third of the time, and if only one-fourth of the student's reading time is at a high level of success, the student will experience only about four minutes of ALT (engaged reading time at a high success level) (Fisher et al., 1978).

Time on task is associated with achievement (Rossmiller, 1982). In some classes engagement rates are regularly under 50 percent, and in others the rates are regularly 90 percent (Fisher et al., 1978). One hour of allocated instruction can result in thirty minutes of actual instruction.

Jane Stallings's studies show that increased time on task in secondary schools leads to improved learning, especially for low-achieving students (AASA, 1982).

The variation in the amount of student-engaged time by achievement groups has been reported by Evertson. On the average, low-achieving junior high students were engaged 40 percent of the time in academic activities, compared with 85 percent engaged time for high-achieving students (Stallings, 1980).

Nancy Karwert noted in a background paper written for the National Commission on Excellence in Education that, although the length of the school year is often 180 days, the amount of time actually devoted to instruction equals about 115 days. Students are frequently found engaged in homeroom exercises, assemblies, class changes, lunch hours, class organization, student conduct, interruptions, and administrative processes (Justiz, 1984).

Questions and Tasks

1. A wealth of educational research has been produced between 1976 and 1986 that is relevant to the improvement of instruction. Through which main source (group) has it caused change in the educational community? After answering, comment on this situation.

2. Paraphrase and interpret Susan Rosenholtz's statement.

3. Do you agree with the findings of Good and Brophy as to teachers' association with low-performing students? What will you do to prevent this from happening in your classroom?

4. In reference to the report by Fisher and others pertaining to emphasis on academic goals, do you think a teacher can be goal oriented and businesslike and at the same time not be "cold"? Explain your answer.

5. On which factors should a teacher's efficiency be evaluated? Speak to this question and the findings of Soar's study.

6. Reread the research under "Consequences." Which study is most difficult for you to accept? Why?

7. Reread the studies under "Instructional Methods" and respond to the following questions.
   a. What is the meaning of "direct" teaching?
   b. Are direct teachers necessarily cold and unsympathetic? Comment.
   c. Does Stallings's study mean that puzzles and games should not be used in the classroom? Explain.
   d. What do we know about the importance of instructional objectives, structuring the lesson, and teachers stating their expectations about the quality of work?
   e. What is the meaning of "active" teaching?

8. Reread the "Seatwork" studies and answer the following.
   a. How much time are students spending on seatwork? What is your opinion of this time?
   b. Are students usually more on task (engaged) during seatwork or when the teacher is conducting a lecture and discussion? Does your answer mean that the other method is inappropriate? Explain your answer.

79

    c. What is a characteristic of a successful manager of seatwork?

9. Why should a teacher limit his or her contact to twenty to thirty seconds while monitoring seatwork?

10. Reread the studies on "Time Allocations" and "Time on Task." Does allocating more instructional time necessarily produce greater student achievement? Explain.

11. Reread the "Managerial" studies and list ten characteristics of effective teachers.

12. In keeping with the results of research, list four approaches that help hold students accountable.

13. We, as teachers, appreciate carpeting, windows, and nicely decorated classrooms, but what is the only physical variable that has been linked to differences in school achievement?

14. Where will you seat your four students who most frequently require monitoring? Provide your answer by placing four X's in each seating arrangement.

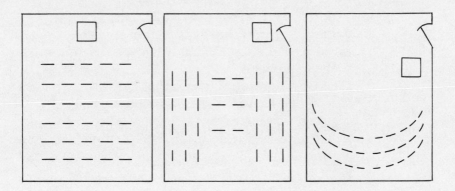

15. Name five things that teachers should do relating to classroom rules.

16. Name three approaches often used by ineffective teachers.

4

The Use of Research to Improve Instruction: Time on Task

Introduction

During recent years, research has provided educators with numerous characteristics of effective teachers. But we continue to largely disregard these findings by using unproven traits as the basis for training, supervising, and evaluating teachers. One variable which research has proven to be characteristic of effective teachers, as pointed out in the previous chapter, is that of time on task. Researchers have concluded that effective teachers directly emphasize academic activities and devote more class time to academic skills. John Goodlad, in his book *A Place Called School*, calls the readers' attention to some schools being unaware "that time is virtually the most precious learning resource they have at their disposal." He further states that "school-to-school differences in using time create inequities in opportunity to learn" (1984, p. 30).

The amount of time students spend on worthy tasks is not only related to their gains in achievement; it is also a determining factor in the teacher's ability to manage the classroom—a prerequisite for successfully implementing almost all pedagogical skills and methods. If we accept these statements as truths, it becomes imperative that teachers be conscious of their engagement rates (the percentage of time a class is on task), be offered suggestions for improvement, and thus become more effective.

Students may become unengaged because of their lack of interest, inabilities, frustration, and the inefficiency of teachers, but considerable time is also lost because of factors such as tardies, absences, collecting money, assemblies, announcements, pull-outs, and overextended recesses. One can better conceptualize the great difference between the time allocated for instruction during a year with the actual time two students may spend on task by studying figure 4.1 (adapted from Karweit, 1983, p. 83). When comparing the *hypothetical* students, one finds the first student absent every sixth day (30 out of 180 days) and averaging a loss of fifteen minutes per hour on his or her attendance days for administrative and organizational activities such as assemblies, announcements, and roll taking. The first student is left with 675 hours out of the initially allocated time of 1,080 hours. Should this student have a teacher who allows him or her to be off task 60 percent of the remaining instructional time, then he or she finally is on task only 270 hours for the complete year. In sharp contrast, the second student benefits from 650 hours of being on task, and undoubtedly his or her achievement will be positively correlated to his or her time on task.

This chapter provides the concerned teacher and supervisors of teachers with the few materials necessary for learning how to determine engagement rates within the confines of a teacher's classroom. (The materials and procedures used are modifications of those developed by Research for Better Schools, Inc., 444 North Third Street, Philadelphia, PA 19123.) With a little practice, a teacher can train a colleague and the two can then become a team. They can visit each other's classroom, make recordings of student behavior, determine the engagement rate, and finally discuss ways to improve students' time on worthy tasks.

Before considering the specific analytical steps for determining a teacher's engagement rate, one needs to realize that there is no specific engagement rate (ER) that separates effectiveness from ineffectiveness. The objective of this procedure is to increase the time on worthy tasks while maintaining a pleasant learning environment. We do not want our children in a classroom with an engagement rate of 100 percent—nor is such an unrealistic goal possible—but we also do not want our children in rooms with rates of 40 percent. As teachers, we should be concerned if our engagement rate is under 65 percent, and we should try to improve it to 80 or 85 percent. The objective is to improve our effectiveness so that students' achievement will improve. There is no "right" engage-

TABLE 4.1

HYPOTHETICAL TIME USAGE

Time Reduced By:

ALLOCATED TIME	Hours Of Attendance	Administrative & Organizational Factors	**Off Task During Instruction	TIME ON TASK
1080 Hours (180 days x 6 hrs)	Student #1 900 Hours (150 days x 6 mos.)	675 Hours (900 hrs. x 15 min. = 225 hrs.)	60% Off 40% On	270
	Student #2 1020 Hours (170 days x 6 hrs.)	765 Hours (1020 hrs. x 15 min. = 255 hrs.)	15% Off 85% On	650

*Examples: collecting money, tardies, assemblies, being unorganized, changing classrooms, pull-outs, teachers' meetings, fire drills, announcements, starting late, etc.

**Examples: socializing, management/transition, disciplining, unoccupied, out of room, waiting for the teacher, etc.

ment rate, and different types of classes and instructional goals may, and should, influence the engagement rates.

Terms

Trainees must conceptualize three terms in order to comprehend and analyze time on task in the classroom: *allocated time, engaged time,* and *engagement rate.*

Allocated time

This is the time allocated to the teaching of a particular subject. The allocated time may be fifty minutes daily for teaching geometry, twenty minutes for penmanship, and ninety minutes for a woodworking laboratory.

Engaged time

Engaged time is that portion of the allocated time during which the student is actually working on or paying attention to the assigned task. Students in one geometry teacher's class may be engaged for forty-three minutes (85 percent of a fifty-minute class), while students in another teacher's class may be engaged for only twenty-four minutes (48 percent). The engaged time is determined by an observer periodically recording on a time-on-task data sheet (figure 4.2) whether students are engaged or unengaged.

Engagement rate

This is the percentage of assigned students who are engaged and on the assigned tasks. Determining the engagement rate requires extracting the number of engaged and unengaged students for each observation from the time on task data sheet and recording the information on the engagement rate form (figure 4.3). The actual engagement rate percentage is then calculated by dividing the number of *assigned* students into the number of *engaged* students.

FIGURE 4.2 *Time on task data sheet.*

Date: _____

Teacher: _____

Observer: _____

School: _____

Class:

(Show seating of students)

Time:
Students assigned:
Pull-Outs:

Engaged: _____
    On subject: _____
    On other assigned
    activities: _____

Unengaged: _____
    Management/
    transition: _____
    Socializing: _____
    Discipline: _____
    Unoccupied/
    observing: _____
    Out of room: _____

Unengaged categories

The observer's primary task, when attempting to determine a teacher's engagement rate, is to periodically observe each student and to record whether he or she is engaged or unengaged. The observer will designate students who are *engaged* by placing an "E" in a space on the time on task data sheet that corresponds to each student's seating assignment.

Students found to be *unengaged*—not involved in the assigned task—are designated on the data sheet by the appropriate category of their unengaged behavior. The five categories of unengaged behavior are indicated below. If the observer is recording while one

FIGURE 4.3

ENGAGEMENT RATE FORM

Date: _____

Teacher: _____

Coder: _____

School: _____

Class: _____

TIME	1	2	3	4	5	TOTAL
ASSIGNED						
ENGAGED						
MANAGEMENT/ TRANSITION						
SOCIALIZING						
DISCIPLINE						
UNOCCUPIED/ OBSERVING						
OUT OF ROOM						

(The rows MANAGEMENT/TRANSITION, SOCIALIZING, DISCIPLINE, UNOCCUPIED/OBSERVING, and OUT OF ROOM are grouped under the label UNENGAGED.)

Calculate the engagement rate for the class by dividing the total number of student engaged by the total number of students assigned.

Engagement rate $= \dfrac{\text{Total students engaged}}{\text{Total students assigned}} =$ _____

Other observations:

Suggestions:

student is rummaging in a desk and another is turning in a completed assignment, then an "M" (management) is recorded for them on the data sheet. Likewise, the observer will record an "S" (socializing) for a student passing a note, a "d" (discipline) for listening to another student being reprimanded, a "U" (unoccupied) for staring out the window, and an "O" (out of the room) for a student who has gone to the restroom.

Unengaged categories

Management/transition (M)
1. Distributing
2. Setting up
3. Gathering equipment and materials
4. "In-between" activities
5. Taking roll, cleaning up, standing in line
6. Listening to nonacademic directions
7. Waiting for teacher's help
8. Turning through pages in book
9. Teacher's directions which do not contain content and are not a disciplining act
10. Student listening to the teacher read answers without explaining
11. Rummaging in desk, sharpening pencil, waiting at teacher's desk, and raising hand.

Socializing (S)
1. Socially interacting
2. Passing notes
3. Laughing, whispering, talking

Disciplining (D)
1. Adult reprimanding a student
2. Student being punished
3. Student watching other student being scolded
4. Head down on desk for punishment

Unoccupied observing (U)
(Student is classified as unoccupied/observing only if he or she cannot be classified in one of the other unengaged categories)
1. Sitting or standing alone
2. Wandering about with no evident purpose
3. Playing with materials
4. Staring out the window

Out of the room (O)
1. Temporarily out of room
2. Errand
3. Bathroom

Procedures

The observer should make an initial visit to the classroom to become acquainted with the room's design, to become familiar with the teacher's lesson plan for the upcoming observation period, and to determine the best place from which to observe.

The observer and teacher should plan at least two or three observation visits. Multiple visits will provide a better overview of the teacher's use of instructional time.

The observer will determine how frequently he or she will code the behavior of each student and the time of the first coding: every five minutes, every ten minutes, or some time in between. The initial coding is predetermined and each coding thereafter is commenced on time. This strictness of procedure is to keep the observer from consciously or unconsciously selecting the best or worse time for coding.

The box on the time on task data sheet (figure 4.4) represents the floor plan, and the lines represent the seats of students who are present. When coding, the observer quickly decides whether a child is *engaged* and if so records an "E" on the student's seat (line). If the student is *unengaged*, the observer determines to which of the five unengaged categories the student's behavior belongs. The appropriate letter is then placed on each line for unengaged students: that is, M, S, D, U, or O.

FIGURE 4.4 *Example of an observer's data sheet.*

					Time:	10:10
E						
E	E	E	E	M	Students assigned:	28
					Pull-outs	1
U	E	O	M	U	Engaged: 17	
E	S	E	E	O	On subject:	17
					On other assigned	
E	E	D	E	E	activities:	0
E	S	E	E	absent	Unengaged: 11	
					Management/transition:	2
	E	U	U	pull-out	Socializing:	2
					Discipline:	1
					Unoccupied/observing:	4
					Out of room:	2

The data sheet entries can be explained as follows:

Time: 10:10	Time of first coding
Students assigned: 28	Number of students present for instruction.
Pull-outs: 1	Students pulled out of this class for remedial instruction, gifted class, etc.
Engaged: 17	Total number engaged. At the prescribed time, the coder in a set sequence observes what each student is doing. If a student is working on an assigned task, he or she is recorded as "E" (engaged).
Number on subject: 17	Number engaged in the subject presently being taught.
Number on other assigned activities: 0	If some students are assigned to work on another subject during the coding time, they are so noted. Example: faster students may finish their reading and start on their math.

Unengaged: 11

If the student is not engaged, then he or she is identified as to the type of unengaged behavior. (See pages 85-88.)

Management transition
(2)
Socializing (2)
Discipline (1)
Unoccupied/observing
(4)
Out of room (2)

The data collected from each of the observations are accumulated on the engagement rate form as depicted below.

FIGURE 4.5 *Sample of Engagement Rate Data*

Time	1 10:10	2 10:18	3 10:26	Total
Assigned	28	29		57
Engaged	17	19		36
Management/ transition	2	0		2
Socializing	2	1		3
Discipline	1	2		3
Unoccupied/ observing	4	5		9
Out of room	2	2		4

(Rows Management/transition through Out of room are grouped under the label **Unengaged**.)

Recalling the definition of engagement rate as being the percentage of assigned students who are engaged and on assigned tasks, the observer or teacher can figure the engagement rate for each classroom visit by extracting two necessary figures from the engagement rate form. The rate is calculated by dividing the *total students assigned* into the *total students engaged*.

$$ER = \frac{\text{Total students engaged}}{\text{Total students assigned}} \quad \frac{36}{57} = 0.63$$

90

As mentioned earlier, there is no one engagement rate that separates the effective teacher from the ineffective teacher, but the percentage provides a gauge for analyzing the amount of time that students are working on assigned tasks. The data on the engagement rate form also provides an overview of the kinds of behaviors in which students are participating when unengaged. This information can be used to develop a list of behaviors and changes that are required for increasing the students' time on task.

One concluding thought about the derived engagement rate number: although the ideal engagement rate is between 0.65 and 0.85, if the students are engaged in worthless instructional tasks, even such a high engagement rate means little. Time is a precious and costly commodity that is not to be wasted—especially on unworthy tasks and assignments.

Learning the importance of educational research, time on task, and how to determine students' engagement rates has marginal value unless the information can be used for instructional improvement. Madeline Hunter says that learning is nearly worthless if it cannot be transferred into new situations. "Learning is like money in the bank; it's great to have it there but it's only useful when you can pull it out and *use* it" (Brandt, 1985, p. 62). *Using* the information already gained in this chapter requires knowing which instructional techniques, if effectively implemented, will result in the more efficient use of instructional time. What specific teaching behaviors are needed to improve the engagement rate? What methods can be employed to increase students' time on task—and therefore their achievement and the teacher's effectiveness? The remainder of this chapter contains a listing of techniques and methods that can be used to answer these questions.

Approaches to Increasing Time on Task

Circulate and check work and work products—keep students accountable.

Don't spend too much time helping one student while losing the remainder of the class.

Avoid disturbing the whole class in the process of correction one student's behavior.

Randomly call on reciters to keep children more attentive and on task.

Have materials ready so that your planning and preparation are not the causes of students being off task.

Be certain that each student has the necessary materials to follow the reader.

Have all students perform in unison.

Require the remainder of the class to read silently while one child reads aloud.

While some students are performing a task at the chalkboard, require the others to do the same task in a workbook or on a ditto sheet.

Use small, individual chalkboards for each student to record and show his or her work.

To keep attention, use new, novel, or varied relevant materials and methods.

Plan for and provide appropriate activities for the early finishers and the "nothing-to-do" students.

Use more frequent shifts of activities as opposed to long periods of just listening, copying, or completing multiple worksheets.

Try not to interfere with children's assigned tasks. (examples: announcements over PA, giving additional directions which should have been given earlier, being overemotional and loud in correcting behavior, irrelevant talk, and so forth).

When correcting a student, consider giving only a simple reprimand instead of a nagging sermon.

Plan and structure the day so that necessary time is not lost because of poor directions, materials not readily accessible, procedures, traffic jams, handing in materials, and so forth.

Structure the transitions between instructional activities so that there are less off-task behaviors.

Realize that long periods of student talk (recitation) result in off-task behavior by other class members.

Consider the time that students spend waiting on the teacher, lining up to exit and enter the room, lining up and waiting to enter the lunchroom, and so forth.

Realize that students who frequently leave their seats to obtain materials are highly susceptible to distractions and tend to be off task more often.

Realize that being overly concerned with students' opinions and allowing students to work on individualized assignments without teacher supervision usually result in a lesser amount of academically engaged time.

Discuss with your principal how and if
—interruptions can be reduced,
—PA announcements can be reduced,
—inappropriate assemblies can be eliminated,
—parents, aids, or secretaries could collect lunch and milk monies,
—students could go to the restroom on their own,
—less time can be spent waiting to enter the lunchroom,
—pull-outs' transition time could be reduced and possibly scheduled for a less critical time or scheduled so that all of a teacher's pull-outs occur only during the corresponding subject period (remedial reading during reading).

Consider the time spent having a student redo work he or she can already do.

Realize that, for some students, fifteen minutes of reading instruction is enough, while others may need an hour.

Realize that busywork types of duplicating sheets may keep students occupied but are not worthy on-task assignments.

Consider integrating or combining subjects into multipurpose lessons. For example, have students *write* a science report or *read* an account of an historical event.

Consider teaming up so that one teacher teaches one level of reading to the whole group while other teachers teach other levels—thus making more appropriate use of instructional time.

Consider shortening or adhering more closely to the time allotted for recess, milk breaks, assemblies, lunch, and so forth.

Is a change in your management needed? Are early finishers and socializing students pulling others off task?

Consider having slower students complete their work during free time or as homework so that other students don't have to wait.

Provide alternative assignments to be completed in order to reduce the unused time students spend waiting for help. Consider the use of peer tutors.

Move around the room regularly and systematically to insure on task behavior.

Make certain that expectations and assignments are clearly stated in behavioral terms.

Require participation by all students in all group activities.

Provide for prerequisite learning needed for a particular task.

Consider the time spent on nonacademic tasks (examples: constructing Christmas wreaths and making May Day baskets in the sixth grade).

Circulate among students to answer questions instead of having students come to the teacher's desk.

Have standards for achievement that are high, yet reasonable.

Give extra tasks and assignments in advance so that the students will stay engaged in academic work after they have finished their first assignment.

Consistently hold students accountable for their work.

Provide a more structured learning environment for students with low pretest scores.

If an overly anxious teacher does not wish to first determine the student engagement rate and then develop a behavior change prescription from the above or some other list of approaches for increasing time on task, he or she may request a colleague or supervisor to measure the amount of time the teacher spends daily on the following fourteen off-task activities (figure 4.6). Almost any teacher will quickly come to realize that he or she can increase the students' time on task and thus their achievement and his or her own effectiveness. Educational research has provided our profession with a basis for improving education—and we, as professionals, should use our own knowledge base.

FIGURE 4.6

Analysis of Off-Task Activities

How many minutes are spent each day:

1. taking roll, collecting money, and attending to other homeroom activities? _____

2. locating, distributing, and collecting materials? _____

3. cleaning up, standing in line, going to the restroom or water? _____

4. reviewing management rulers and giving nonacademic directions? _____

5. reprimanding student(s), thereby causing other students to be disturbed and pulled off task? _____

6. by students being unengaged while waiting for the teacher? _____

7. during which the staff members interfere with children's assigned tasks (examples: engaging in irrelevant talk, giving additional directions, having visitors, announcement over PA, being overemotional and loud in correcting behavior? _____

8. with one (or a few) students while others need assistance? _____

9. during which the teacher is unavailable to assist students (examples: speaking to a visitor, handling emergencies, and being tied up with one group)? _____

10. on activities with marginal or little value to the instructional objectives? _____

11. on lengthy student recitations before the teacher regains "leadership"? _____

12. exceeding the time allotted for recess and lunch? _____

13. allowing pupils to get drinks and go to the restroom during instructional time? _____

14. when students are out of the room, during a lesson, for the convenience of scheduling remedial instruction? _____

15. OTHER

Questions and Tasks

1. In reference to John Goodlad's statement, is time really the "most precious learning resource" that teachers have at their disposal? Justify your answer.

2. In analyzing the "Hypothetical Time Usage" (table 4.1), how many hours would a student be on task if he or she were absent eleven days out of a possible 180 six-hour school days, lost an average of twelve minutes each hour that he or she was in attendance due to tardies, announcements, teachers starting class late, and other similar factors, and the teachers had him or her on task for 64 percent of the instructional periods?

3. What will be the correct engagement rate for you? Explain your answer.

4. Print the correct symbol for identifying into which unengaged categories the following behaviors are classified.

    _____ Waiting for the teacher's help
    _____ Gone to his locker in the hallway
    _____ Passing a note
    _____ Reading the Bible during social studies
    _____ Listening to a peer being reprimanded

5. When determining the engagement rate, why should the observer visit the teacher's classroom before the coding period?

    Why is one coding not enough?

    Why should there be a set sequence for recording the students' behaviors?

    If the unengaged behavior cannot be suitably placed in one of the five categories, how is the behavior coded?

6. What does the engagement rate tell the teacher?

7. Use the list of approaches for increasing time on task to recommend some behaviors and methods for improving the following teacher. List your five most important recommendations.

Name: Pat Guskey

Classes taught: Junior high social studies

Teacher's rating: Receives above-average ratings from both students and supervisors

Teaching format as exemplified by the nine o'clock class:

9:00 - 9:07	The teacher organizers material and takes roll.
9:07 - 9:10	Students are getting materials ready and are slowly getting on task.
9:10 - 9:14	One tardy and one previously absent student arrive and are attended to.
9:10 - 9:16	Teacher introduces today's topic and gives set induction.
9:16 - 9:19	The daily announcements come over the PA system.
9:19 - 9:30	Lecture/discussion: The students' engagement rate is 68 percent.
9:25 - 9:26	A student runner knocks and informs the teacher that John Evans is to see his counselor.
9:30 - 9:33	The teacher provides directions for seatwork.
9:33 - 9:50	Students work on seatwork with an engagement rate of 48 percent.
9:46 - 9:50	A majority of students have put up their materials and are visiting and waiting for the bell by 9:47.

Even though this teacher is well regarded by both the students and the supervisor, would you want your child to be in these classes? Explain your answer.

8. Make arrangements with one of your college professors or some area teacher to visit his or her classroom for the purpose of determining the engagement rate of one of his or her classes. Using the procedures and forms outlined in this chapter, conduct the observations, figure the engagement

rate, and prepare a two-page statement which includes your major observations and recommendations.

5

The Use of Research to Improve Instruction: Getting Ready to Manage Students

Introduction

Although separated by only one wall, two classrooms may be managed by extremely different techniques and with extremely different results.

> Most nine o'clock students in Room 101 are in their chairs prior to the bell and have placed their study materials on their desks' surfaces. There is limited noise, but it ceases with the sounding of the final take-up bell and as the teacher promptly makes eye contact with the class members. The students begin putting the finishing touches on their homework assignment, and others read the posted assignments and then start working on today's objectives. The teacher simultaneously completes the lunch money bookkeeping, acknowledges a student's excuse for being absent, silently takes roll, and has prepared the absentee report by 9:04. Students in Room 101 are found to usually be attentive and respectful, and to have an engagement rate of 83 percent. When given seatwork and homework, most quickly start working and continue to work until the teacher directs them to prepare for the dismissal bell. Students raise their hands before speaking. The teacher is businesslike and task oriented, but also friendly and supportive of the students' efforts.

Next door a colleague has an entirely different approach towards instruction and classroom management—and radically different student behavior.

Students in Room 102 are still laughing and jostling as the take-up bell sounds. The teacher steps into the room only three minutes later and begins to check roll and handle other administrative tasks. At 9:07 the students are directed to get quiet and to get out their books. The teacher starts the presentation at 9:09 and is interrupted three times by tardy students. Several members are found to be attentive and on task, as is verified by the class' engagement rate of 58 percent during the lecture/discussion and 49 percent during seatwork. Students in Room 102 are frequently found socializing and speaking out during the teacher's presentation; most are waiting for the dismissal bell five minutes before it rings. The teacher is friendly and expresses a desire for students to do well.

The two scenarios are similar to those used in the introduction to *Organizing and Managing the Junior High Classroom*, a study conducted by the Research and Development Center for Teacher Education at the University of Texas. The two scenes force one to acknowledge the more effectual teacher and to realize that this teacher most assuredly employs different management techniques than does the second teacher. Do effective managers share some common preparatory managerial approaches, and have they been identified?

The Texas center initiated their study in 1978 to determine "how effective teachers organize and manage their classes from the first days of school and maintain their management effectiveness throughout the year." The investigators studied the teaching behaviors of fifty-one teachers in eleven schools with middle school and junior high grades. At the end of the study the team's descriptive narratives of events, measurements of engagement rates, ratings of teachers' and students' behaviors, and students' achievement test scores were used to identify those teachers and their behaviors which were successful "in establishing and maintaining well-managed classrooms." The findings of the study were used to formulate recommendations on how to effectively organize and manage classrooms. An outlined presentation of some of the investigators' concerns and recommendations follows. Although the procedures may seem overwhelming in number and some may appear trite and insignificant, teachers need to develop all of them to become effective classroom managers. Moreover, learners frequently think they have a grasp of something until they are asked to give specifics or to perform. If you react to each of the following recommendations by explaining *your exact* procedures, you will come to realize that your managerial procedures are often too vague to effectively manage twenty-five students for seven hours each day.

Pre-instructional organization

I. Displays
  A. Plan and prepare for a posting of class rules and consequences.

  B. Allocate board space or poster space for listing the assignments during the week.

  C. Allocate posting space for the day's assignments.

  D. Determine and prepare the room decorations and bulletin boards for the first six weeks of school. Do not overdecorate, and leave space for posting students' work.

II. Furniture and Work Areas
  A. Plan the arrangement of student desks.
      1. It is extremely important, during the initial weeks, that you minimize distractions; therefore, you may wish to temporarily place desks in rows facing the primary instructional areas.
      2. Arrange desks so that you can observe all students and so all students can observe you.
      3. Provide traffic areas to doors, supply areas, paper turn-in stations, chalkboards, and learning centers.
      4. The desk arrangement should allow for constant monitoring with minimal walking. Leave regularly spaced passageways between desks to allow ease in monitoring.

  B. Plan the placement of your desk.
      1. Most teacher's space and desk occupy one-fourth of the classroom's floor space. Possibly some of the space could be better used for student desks or learning centers.

2. Does the teacher's desk need to be located in the front and middle of the room?

C. Audio-visual equipment: notice the location of electrical outlets before locating equipment and instructional areas.

D. Plan work and storage areas.
   1. Location of learning centers should allow eye contact between students and teacher.
   2. Shortage of storage furniture: you may need to use bricks. boards, card tables, cover cloths, and storage boxes in creating your own.
   3. Obtain file folders and begin organizing files by units or topics. File leftover worksheets with their ditto masters.

III. Supplies, Equipment, and Forms
   A. Determine the student supplies that will be required. Which will the district furnish and which will students purchase? What is the procedure for informing parents?

   B. Obtain used cigar boxes, coffee cans, and other containers for rulers, pencils, and other objects.

   C. Place student supplies in an accessible location. The location should be one that produces the least amount of disruptions from movement to and from the area.

   D. Obtain or know the location of readily available extension cords and adaptor plugs.

   E. Determine which audio-visual equipment is available in the school. Determine if there is a checkout procedure or a first come, first served procedure.

   F. Acquaint yourself with routine forms for requesting equipment, field trip transportation, report cards, attendance reports, tardy slips, hall passes, grade book, instructor's manuals, and so forth.

   G. Determine if teachers are responsible for issuing and accounting for students' textbooks. If so, learn the procedure.

Establishing Rules and Procedures

I. Beginning Class
   A. Decide how to handle previously absent students.
       1. Establish a record system. Some use their grade book by recording an "A" for absent and "T" for tardy.
       2. Must students obtain an absence excuse slip from the office or will they offer you the excuse? Will you require students to leave the excuse on your desk or will you ask them for it?

   B. Tardy students: is there a schoolwide consequence for tardy students? If not, develop your own. Some schools and teachers issue detentions for tardy students.

   C. Decide on procedures for take-up bell and initial minutes.
       1. Communicate expectations.
           a. Shall there be no talking or soft talking? Shall they begin work or wait? Begin work on what?
           b. Which supplies should students have available and ready for use: sharpened pencil, homework, heading on papers, textbooks?
           c. Specifically state and post what students are to do while you are attending to clerical duties such as checking out textbooks.
       2. Develop a system for distributing supplies.
           a. Will you distribute, have each student pick up his own, or will assistants pass them out? Will each be handed one or will they be passed down seat rows?
           b. When possible, give directions and a demonstration before passing out materials. Consider posting the directions.

II. Procedures during Instruction
   A. Decide how students are to contact you.
       1. Most teachers require a raised hand.
       2. Will you go to students' desks or will they come to you? Do not allow students to wait at your desk.

   B. Decide how to handle students leaving their seats.
       1. Specify for what reasons they may get up. Is permission necessary for sharpening a pencil, turning in

papers, coming to your desk, leaving the room, and so forth?

2. What is the procedure for students going to the library, office, lockers, and restrooms?

    a. This procedure must be established early and consistently followed.

    b. Students should normally leave the room only for emergencies. Passing periods and recesses are normally sufficient time for going to lockers, getting drinks, and so forth.

C. What signal will you use to capture the students' attention?

1. Teachers usually use a particular signal to let students know they are ready to begin a presentation.

2. Some techniques are ringing a small bell, sitting down in a predesignated place, standing in a particular spot by the chalkboard, and statements such as "Let me have your attention."

D. Establish heading for papers.

1. Thoroughly explain this before the first assignment.

2. Prepare and post an enlarged example for all to see until the behavior is established.

E. Establish rules for talking during seatwork.

1. Can students quietly talk during seatwork? If talking gets too loud will the privilege be immediately lost?

2. Can students work together during seatwork? Are there restrictions and consequences?

3. If quiet talking or group work is allowed, *active* monitoring is still necessary.

F. Decide how to handle early finishers.

1. What do early finishers do?

2. Have a wide assortment of worthwhile enrichment and extension activities.

    a. Is extra credit awarded for completing an additional task?

    b. Can two or more students work simultaneously on an activity?

     c. Where will the materials be kept and what procedure is there for returning materials?

  G. Establish rules for lab and project work.

    1. What safety rules need to be explained—and repeated?

    2. Will students work alone, in pairs, or threes? What variable will be used to group students? Attempt to insure full participation by having each student record the group's work. Evaluate *each* student's work.

    3. What conduct rules will be in force regarding talking, movement, and sharing of materials?

    4. What supplies are needed and how are they to be distributed?

    5. How will you insure enough cleanup time? Who is responsible for which duties?

III. Ending the Class

  A. What procedure is there for putting items away? Does each student return the items, do monitors pick them up, or are they passed forward?

  B. Are there folders and containers available for filing each class's work?

  C. Is there a standard of neatness before students can leave their desk areas and work spaces?

  D. Do you have a procedure for dismissal? Must all students be in their seats and quiet before being dismissed?

Student Accountability

I. Seatwork and Homework

  A. Determine headings and remind students several times during the initial weeks. Tell them the consequences (for example, 3 points off assignment grade).

  B. Work materials: can students use paper that frays when being removed from spiral notebooks, pencil or pen, write on back, and how stringent as to legibility?

C. Incomplete work: will you grade incomplete work or must it be complete?
  1. Pay attention at the beginning of the year that the assigned work is completed.
  2. Counsel with each student the first time he or she fails to turn in an assignment.
  3. Call a parent when a child is remiss with two consecutive assignments. Remain friendly and encouraging, but insist on completed work.

D. Make due dates reasonable and clear but impose a penalty for late work unless it is accompanied by a parent's excuse.

E. Assignments should be orally explained and then posted or presented in a syllabus. The posting can later save explanations in getting students on task by simply referring to the posted assignments.

F. Determine grading criteria and the weight of each criterion for specific assignments.

II. Monitoring
  A. Instantaneously begin walking to see that each student is started and can do the work. Continue to monitor throughout the period.

  B. It is desirable to have students begin homework in class by leading the class in completing the first few problems or questions.

  C. Maintain with-it-ness: look around the room at frequent intervals even when occupied with other matters.

  D. During recitation and class discussions, have *all* students participate.

III. Student Evaluators
  A. Assignments with clearly defined answers can be expeditiously checked by students exchanging papers.

  B. This method provides quick feedback.

  C. It also saves teacher's time.

  D. Determine in advance how papers are to be exchanged.

E. This method may encourage cheating.
1. Have graders put their names in the upper left corner and the number missed underneath their names.
2. Take up the papers, check accuracy of graders, and record the grades.

IV. Academic Feedback
A. Be certain that your grading scale (percentages) is consistent with school policy.

B. Determine and communicate the components and relative values upon which the final grade will be based: daily assignments, papers, projects, tests, quizzes, participation, contributions, critical thinking, worksheets, notebook, and extra credit work.

C. Encourage students to maintain a record of their grades. The issuance of a simple record sheet with spaces for name of work, date, and grade will encourage their participation.

D. Some teachers maintain wall posters which indicate each student's mastery of objectives and assignments completed.

E. Decide on procedures for long-term projects:
1. Discourage last-minute efforts by periodically checking each student's progress.
2. Some teachers predetermine various levels of completeness and then treat each portion as a miniassignment. Naturally, specifics and due dates are initially explained.

You have probably come to realize that the majority of the recommendations growing out of the Texas study are not unique and that, regardless of whether teachers know of the study, they are likely to implement these recommendations as they gain experience through the trial-and-error method. Trial and error is an effective method of learning, but it also takes a toll in frustration and in the loss of a professional's time. Again, research findings are available and can be used to train and produce not just teachers, but efficient teachers.

Questions and Tasks

1. Reread the two scenarios while visualizing the two teachers. What is the teacher in Room 102 lacking? What are the two teachers' convictions toward learning?

2. Since you will soon be managing a classroom, outline your exact procedures for implementing the recommendations presented in this chapter.

3. At this time, review the classroom rules and consequences that you developed when studying Assertive Discipline. Would you now care to change any parts? If so, how?

4. Using the recommendations, present two different furniture arrangements for your future classroom.

5. Obtain a page from a grade book. How will you enter tardies, excused absences, and unexcused absences?

6. When you were in the eighth grade did you present your absent excuse to the office or to your teachers? If you were now a principal, what would be your school's procedure for dealing with tardies and absences?

7. What procedures do you plan to use in the following:

    A. Distributing tests
    B. Picking up homework
    C. Distributing supplies
    D. Issuing books at the start of the year

8. Answer the following:

    A. When will you arrive for your 8:30 class?
    B. What will students do upon entering the classroom?
    C. What will students do while you are tending to clerical and administrative chores?
    D. What will be your procedure for pulling the class's attention to you?

9. How many students will be allowed on the floor at any one time? Will your answer be the same for lectures, seatwork, and lab work? Why?

10. May students leave your classroom for drinks, restrooms, and lockers? Explain your rules and procedures.

11. Read elsewhere about with-it-ness. Describe one of your previous teachers who did *not* have this ability.

Part III

Additional Managerial Concerns, Methods, and Resources

6

Routine Managerial Concerns and Methods

Teachers are frequently engaged in as many as one thousand interpersonal exchanges during one six-hour day. (Alvord and Glass, 1974). This knowledge, along with the realization that these exchanges take place simultaneously with twenty to thirty students from various cultures, at various achievement levels, with varying types of interests (and lack of interests), with varying physical restraints and at various levels of hyperactivity and emotional depressions, makes teaching effectiveness appear to be a near impossibility. But it is a near impossibility only if the teacher does not know the numerous interpersonal skills and pedagogical methods characteristic of effective classroom managers. Although numerous research-proven skills, traits, methods, and managerial models have been presented, there are some routine managerial skills that deserve further discussion. Since some of these have been touched upon in earlier chapters, you can use the index and chapter references to gain more information on these topics.

Body language and vocal cues

Our body movement, gestures, and voice can have a profound effect on how students perceive our wishes, and the reverse is also true. We should become cognizant of body language expressions and vocal cues for three reasons: to better communicate our managerial desires to students; to develop communication skills that are independent of the voice and are therefore less disruptive to the learning environment; and to better understand students' feelings by being able to read their body movements and vocal cues.

Regardless of a teacher's or a student's words, anger can be detected from a voice that is loud, of high pitch, irregularly inflected up and down, and rapid (Knapp, 1972). Frequently our facial expressions and body posture are very expressive. A smile tells another person that our words are probably not serious, just as a wink or laughter, immediately preceding a story, tells the listener that the speaker's words are to be taken lightly (Scheflen, 1972, p. 73).

Tension, even without words, can often be easily detected. The suppressed anger of a teacher or student may be revealed by retracted shoulders, whereas fear may be indicated by raised shoulders. Other body expressions are as follows:

Body expressions	Feelings
Leaning forward	Preparing to protest
Pointed forefinger	Wanting to rebuke
Many leg movements	Depressions
Moving small objects	Discomfort or tenseness
Frequent hand to nose	Fear
Closed fist	Aggression

Although the above body movements do not show a perfect correlation to every student's feelings, "they are general indices to which the teacher can refer to recognize the emotional states of students' and they are also indicators of the emotional states of teachers" (Project T.E.A.C.H., n.d., p. 17).

Teachers' and parents' eyes can be great communicators in regulating youths' behavior. You may recall a parent or teacher whose eye contact forced you into compliance. Likewise, if we look away during a student's explanation, we may communicate that we are not interested or that we do not agree with what is being said. Most cultural groups tend to make more eye contact with those who are supportive, but this is not true of all groups and societies. Teachers often use eye contact as a signal for listening, responding, and attention, but this skill is not a natural behavior for beginning teachers—it must be practiced before it can be used effectively (Charles, 1985, p. 90). Effective teachers are noted for being able to make eye contact with *all* students—not just the select, attentive ones. The teacher who "deliberately seeks the eyes of all students, will better be able to create the positive, interested attitudes desired" (Project T.E.A.C.H., n.d., p. 23).

Although most mainland teachers in our nation's schools desire eye contact from their students, it is unnatural for some children to comply. A teacher who insists on eye contact from a child whose culture has taught him or her to look down when being addressed by an adult will probably develop a confrontation rather than gain the child's attention. It therefore behooves teachers to become acquainted with, and respectful of, their students' cultures and values.

Force

The adage to "never say never" is barely acceptable when applied to the use of brute force upon a student. The only occasion when physical restraint or "wrestling" may be justified would be the rare instance when it is necessary to protect oneself from the actions of an out-of-control student. Even in these instances, it is best, if possible, to send for your supervisor or principal and to allow that individual, as a third party, to calm or remove the student. Teachers are not paid to wrestle or physically force students, and courts often rule the force employed in these situations to be excessive. Moreover, you will lose less status by informing the enraged, abusive, or defiant student that the matter will be dealt with later, after a cooling period, than by pinning the youth to the floor or carrying him or her out of the classroom.

Rule of Thumb: Do not put your hands on a student when you are disturbed with a child's behavior, nor when a student is disturbed by your treatment of him or her.

Life space and touching

Physical encounters are less likely if teachers remain sensitive to the life space or intimate distance of their students—especially the life space of the emotionally disturbed child who feels unfairly treated. Should a student become fearful of your presence, it is prudent to not impinge into his or her life space, a space minimally

115

surrounding the individual by four feet, for he or she may feel forced into a "flight or fight" situation. Neither of these two perceived options by the student is desired, therefore, attempt to prevent both by remaining outside the student's life space zone. In highly volatile situations, instead of using force on the upset student, it is better to provide a calming period by informing the child in a nonthreatening manner that you will talk later, and then return to the lesson. During this period you can also reflect on why the child "blew up," and then treat the incident more as a problem to be solved than an act to be punished. Should the student choose "flight," do not attempt to block his or her exit or to forcibly restrain the student from leaving the classroom. But upon that exit, seek assistance from the office.

Some teachers have been able to use touch to nonverbally convey feelings of approval or to communicate a need for a student to "settle down." But other educators have found students to perceive such "gestures as an invasion of privacy" (Project T.E.A.C.H., n.d., p. 22). Not only do some feel their privacy to have been invaded; sometimes parents and courts will frown on such practices, especially if the act is perceived by a complaining child to be one of intimacy. These occurrences are more likely to result when male teachers are involved. Furthermore, society is discriminatory in that it allows women more freedom to touch students than it extends to men.

Firmness versus roughness, sarcasm, and criticism

Effective teachers, those who lose minimal instructional time dealing with disruptive behavior, express an attitude of firmness. Students know that these teachers' messages always convey "I mean it—now." Students respond as quickly to firm, "matter of fact" directions, stated in normal speech, as to rough and loud demands. Teachers who use firmness stand in contrast to harsh teachers, who seemingly believe that the emotional context and loudness of their message will increase compliance. But research does not support the rough teachers' practices. In fact, not only do they not significantly improve compliance, but the harsh and loud commands actually produce less task involvement by their disturbing influence on the other class members. *Rough* teachers usually cause much more off-task behavior than do the misbehaving children.

Most educators recognize the existing relation between students' self-concept and school performance: that is, students with a positive self-concept tend to be more motivated to achieve. Knowing this, it is incumbent on teachers to refrain from using sarcasm concerning the child's personality.

> Disapproval and criticism are more likely to be respected when they do not threaten self-concept, when they are accompanied by positive expectations, and when they speak to the situation rather than the personalities. (Project T.E.A.C.H., n.d., p. 11)

Teachers who sincerely care about their students attack the problem rather than the student (Ginott, 1972).

Low-profile control

Teachers who use low-profile control stand in direct contrast to those who shout, use sarcasm, and draw attention to misbehaving students. Carl Rinne (1982, p. 53) describes the low-profile teacher as one who does not use "conventional classroom control or high profile." The high-profile teacher, after telling the students, "Now on page 26, you should do the problem," might loudly command Johnny to stop looking out the window instead of doing his work assignment. This approach may embarrass Johnny and make him resentful of the teacher's ridicule, or he may graciously accept the command and get on task without any resentment. But even if the result is the latter, the high-profile teacher has significantly disturbed other students. The low-profile teacher, noticing Johnny looking out the window, might add, "All of you, including Ann, Johnny, Bruce, and Sarah, can look at the graph at the bottom of page 26." We notice that this low-profile teacher's method was to direct the students' attention to the lesson while trying to not pull the other children off task. This teacher's smooth, low-keyed directive will go virtually unnoticed by everyone except the off-task Johnny, who distinctly heard his name and the message. The same low-profile teacher will frequently move around the room monitoring students rather than being seated at the desk and then shouting at students to get back on task.

117

Rules

Since the primary purpose of teaching is to instill learning, an orderly environment with minimal disruptions must be created and maintained. If common classroom rules are not imposed by school policy, individual teachers must identify what student behaviors they need to maintain an orderly learning environment. The many behaviors that a teacher both desires and loathe are too numerous to effectively monitor and enforce. They are so numerous in fact, that one's list must be reduced to the most important and then grouped into three to five rules that will be *consistently* enforced.

Frederic Jones (1979, p. 27) found that over 90 percent of classroom disruptions were caused by students either talking or walking (movement), and most teachers' rules include procedures for regulating both. Below was one teacher's initial list of rules which was later reduced to five rules and thoroughly explained, modeled, and posted.

Follow directions.
Complete all assignments.
Work independently.
Raise hand before speaking.
Be in class on time.
Do not leave the room without permission.
Keep hands, feet, and objects to oneself.
Bring books, pen, and paper to class.

Obtain permission before leaving your chair.
No cussing or teasing.
Be polite and helpful.
Respect others' property.
Do not hit, shove, or hurt others.
Don't interrupt the teacher or other students when they are talking.

Since a list of five rules cannot cover all aspects of behavior, teachers will occasionally need to temporarily replace the general rules with different ones for specific activities. For instance, "No talking without permission" may be temporarily replaced with "Quiet, constructive talking allowed during group work."

Good classroom rules must be reasonable, observable, and enforceable—as discussed earlier in the chapters on contingency management, reality therapy, and assertive discipline. Once the rules are identified, they should be posted in a highly visible location. Each posted rule must be explained with concrete examples that communicate to students what the rule means. A concluding emphatic directive on this discussion of rules: do not waste your time identifying, posting, and explaining rules unless you will *consistently* enforce them. Effective teachers are consistent in holding students accountable for both academic achievement and good conduct. They do not become lax on their "high days" and then expect automatic compliance when their own and their students' moods and behaviors require more adherence to the previously established rules.

Consequences

Teachers who have high status among students often manage their students' behavior by praising and giving attention to well-behaved and on-task students. Some management models employ less positive consequences, as was illustrated in the previous discussions on Dreikurs's mistaken goal model, Jones's management training, and assertive discipline. Consequences that promote behaviors are termed "reinforcers," or "reinforcing stimuli." As was discussed under contingency management, reinforcers are exemplified by rewards and the cessation of unpleasant and painful events. Those consequences that weaken behaviors are called "punishers." Punishers are exemplified by the cessation of rewarding events or the use of behavior that causes pain (Becker, Engelmann, and Thomas, 1971, p. 16).

Although most teachers use intermediate variations, some teachers largely use reinforcing consequences—stimuli that increase the probability of future occurrences of desirable behavior. These teachers continually look for and compliment good behavior and may have formal reward systems. Other teachers attempt to manage classrooms largely by punishing—by using techniques that decrease the probability of the future occurrence of some undesired behavior. Teachers who are grouped as punishers often do not have a planned management system and expect to manage by fear—fear by their students that inappropriate conduct will result in a painful retaliation for violation of the teacher's wish.

When possible, consequences should be closely related to the rule which was broken. If Sara threw gum in the hallway, it would be appropriate to have her pick it up, clean the hallway (during nonin-

Consequences: Examples of Reinforcers and Punishers*

Little effort required

- Maintaining eye contact (until the behavior stops)
- Asking the student to state the rule he or she has broken
- Telling the child to stop the behavior
- Putting the child last in line or waiting to go to lunch or recess
- Giving the child a chance to change seats if he or she feels tempted to misbehave
- Telling the child what you expect him or her to be doing
- Smiling
- Patting the child on the back
- Giving a cheery note on an assignment
- Letting the child go first to lunch or recess or be first in line
- Letting the child be a teacher's aide
- Letting the best table or row go to lunch or recess first

Some effort required

- Arranging a short conference with the child
- Having the child stay after school
- Withdrawing a privilege
- Calling parents
- Not allowing the child to play at recess
- Sending a negative note to parents
- Semi-isolating the child within the room
- Denying a regular class treat (such as a trip to the library, a popcorn party)
- Giving a happy face or star
- Sending a positive note to parents
- Issuing an individual award certificate
- Giving a reward time for games, free play, or a favorite activity
- Putting the child's name on a Superstar list on the board
- Giving a special art activity prizes (such as pencils, erasers)
- Giving a pass for the library

Much effort required

- Denying a major class treat, such as a field trip
- Going to the principal's office
- Administering corporal punishment
- Organizing a behavior modification program
- Drawing up a behavior contract
- Arranging for a field trip, party, or other special group activity
- Passing out tokens which students can collect and "cash in" for privileges or special treats

*Modification of Evertson et al., 1981, pp. 60-61.

structional time), or apologize to the custodian for messing up the school. These consequences would be more appropriate than having her write thirty times, "Sara will dispose of her gum by wrapping it and placing it in the trash can" or by being sent to the principal. Curwin and Mendler (1980, pp. 117-122) recognize this need for consequences to relate to the broken rules, and add that consequences should be administered, when possible, immediately after the rule is broken.

Hierarchical consequences

Some teachers establish a graduated series of consequences that are imposed on rule violators in a set sequence. Other teachers spontaneously select which consequence will be imposed. A teacher employing the graduated or hierarchical series of consequences might have adopted a managerial system similar to Canters' assertive discipline system, in which each violation has a specific consequence that all students know about in advance. For example, see the following (Curwin and Mendler, 1980, p. 120):

Rule: *Students will be in class on time.*
Consequences:
   1st   infraction = each six-week period the first infraction results in a teacher-student conference
   2nd   infraction = student will make up lost time during recess, lunch, or after school
   3rd   infraction = student will make up double the lost time
   4th   infraction = parents will be contacted and tardiness will be discussed (withdrawal of home privilege will be recommended)
   5th   infraction = the fifth infraction and each one thereafter results in the loss of one point toward the grading period.

The fifth infraction is reluctantly presented as a possible consequence. Courts frown on schools using grades as punishment to correct disciplinary behavior, especially when points or grades are taken away from previously earned grades.

Punishment

"Substitute teachers abhor situations in which they must teach a class that has been controlled almost exclusively by fear of punishment," for as soon as the students realize that the substitute is not a punisher, "deviances appear in profusion" (Boules, 1981, p. 140). Researchers have found that although punishment may suppress deviant behavior, it does not weaken the attitude or need which lies beneath the behavior. Simply put, research indicates that punishment, especially physical punishment, is notably ineffective as a socialization method. This is not to say that mild punishment is never appropriate, but that the following weaknesses are recognized:

1. "The effect of punishment has been shown to last a short time" (Buckley and Walker, 1978, p. 47). Part of the reason may be that it is too often dispensed inconsistently, according to teachers' moods.
2. The behavior behind punishment is often suppressed only in the presence of the punisher.
3. Sometimes what is perceived by the teacher to be punishment is reinforcing to a misbehaving youth in that he or she has succeeded in annoying the teacher, has received the attention of all his or her peers and the teacher, and has therefore usurped the teacher's power by controlling the teacher.
4. If the punishment is viewed by the recipient as being unwarranted or excessive, the resulting feeling may produce a learning withdrawal or a devious counterattack on the teacher.

When punishment is used, the person administering the act should be regulated by the following guidelines:

1. Determine if the child actually knew the correct behavior.
2. Did the teacher model the correct behavior earlier?
3. Punishment should be applied promptly.
4. Punishments should be applied consistently, not whimsically.
5. Punishment should be fairly applied to all students.
6. The punishing act should not violate school and district policies, nor state statutes.
7. Harsh punishment should be infrequent. If otherwise, the teacher's proficiency should be questioned.

8. Punishment should be mild and impersonal.
9. The punisher should not be emotionally upset while administering the punishment.

It is also important to not use mass punishment. As tempting as it sometimes is, especially for teachers who are lacking in procedural alternatives, mass punishment is not fair. It is not right to force punctuality by having the whole class remain fifteen minutes after class or by assigning additional homework because one class member arrived late. Likewise, it is not correct to punish, assign more work, or deduct points from everyone because one, four, or fifteen students are talking, cheating, or tardy.

Transitions

Transition is defined here as "the time and routine involved in changing from one activity to another." In effective teachers' classrooms, routine transitions may be no greater than thirty seconds, virtually all students are punctual in getting ready for the next activity, and there is little, if any, misbehavior during the transition period. Less effective managers are frequently found to spend four to nine minutes between activities, during which time there is frequently misbehavior and the teacher frequently begins the new activity with some students inattentive and unprepared—off task.

Elementary classrooms, counting start-up and dismissals, may have eight to twelve planned transitions each day. Secondary teachers frequently must manage three or four transitions per period (hour). The importance of smooth transitions for academic focus and time-on-task can be realized by comparing nine transitions of five-minute duration with nine transitions of thirty-second duration. In a year's time, less effective managers might spend 127 1/2 hours, or the equivalent of 21¼ six-hour instructional days, in changing activities, getting ready, and dismissing classes. For the teacher who routinely spends thirty seconds per transition, only 12¾ hours per year (170 days), or the equivalent of 2⅛ six-hour instructional days, would be spent on transitions. Most of us would agree on which teacher we would prefer for our child—all other skills being equal.

Smooth, quick transitions "do not just happen" or are a result of a teacher always getting the "good kids." Instead, they are a result of students following rules of transition that have been identified, discussed, modeled, and then consistently adhered to. In addition, smooth and quick transitions are fortified by the teacher having been thoroughly prepared for the coming activity and monitoring students' behavior during this time, rather than hunting for his or her resource book, sorting ditto papers, or spending several minutes with his or her back turned, writing subject matter on the chalkboard. The prepared teacher also invites cooperation by praising desired behavior with statements such as "Good, Beth, you are following the transition rules" and "Bill, that's terrific. You are one of the first ones ready to start your seatwork."

Stan Paine and his associates (1983, p. 85) advocate listing, discussing, posting, and adhering to four transition rules:

1. Move quietly.
2. Put your books away and get what you need for the next activity.
3. If necessary, move your chair quietly.
4. Keep your hands and feet to yourself.

The second step may require an explanation of what the activity will be and what materials are needed. This is most true at the beginning of the school year and for nonroutine activities thereafter. Teachers often signal transition times by saying "It's time for math" or "It's transition time" and "You will see posted on the board our next assignment," plus any other necessary remarks.

Desist techniques

A desist is an action that a teacher takes to immediately suppress misbehavior, thus allowing the lesson to continue. Desists may be in the form of an unapproving facial expression, a verbal directive, or some other form of punishment. Teachers recognize as ineffective disciplinarians are often found to be overly dependent on desist techniques, to use little variety, to feel a need to employ desists too frequently, and to progressively become overly forceful in their usage. Effective managers use desists sparingly; however, both types of teachers are frequently found to show too little variety.

The limitation of having too few desist options may precipitate the teacher and the misbehaver into unnecessary confrontations. For example, when a teacher's only managerial techniques are those of loudly calling a student's name, having the student put his or her head on the desk, or sending the student to the office, that teacher quickly runs out of options and often becomes more of a disruptive influence on the lesson than does the behavior of the disruptive child. Frequently used desists are also found to have a diminishing effect, and teachers tend to compensate for the "effectiveness loss" by increasing the forcefullness of the desist. This may explain why teachers who loudly scold become progressively louder until they reach a yelling point.

Carl and LaDonna Wallen (1978, p. 213) believe that teachers should consider the many rewarding and punishing consequences (desists) and their uses by making an extensive list and then placing the desist techniques on "stair steps" from minimum to maximum forcefulness (see Figure 6.1). This placement is to aid in analysis and is not meant to imply that a misbehaving student is to be given all of the "steps."

The manner in which teachers deploy desists will partially determine their effectiveness. As discussed earlier, teachers should not yell but should project firmness in what they say. Desists should also be dispensed calmly, consistently, and punctually.

The type of consequence and how it is dispensed greatly influences how disruptive it is to the lesson and the effect it has on other students—its "ripple effect." The research of Jacob Kounin found that the ripple effect may be affected, in varying degrees, by characteristics of the desist act: clarity, firmness, and roughness. When the desist's clarity identified the deviate's name and the unacceptable behavior, student witnesses to the incident tended to increase their conforming behavior. Firmness, the holding of an "I-mean-it" attitude until the deviant behaved, increased the conformity of the misbehaver but not of the student witnesses. Roughness (anger, threats, and physical punishment) did not improve behavior (Kounin, 1970).

The ripple effect is not as significant at the high school level as it is at the elementary school level. A high school study found the type of desist used had little influence on the amount of behavior exhibited by the student witnesses. An exception to this finding was that an extremely angry outburst caused some emotional discom-

FIGURE 6.1

List of Desists

Establish eye contact
Frown at student
Shake your head
Move closer to student
Gently place hand on student
Write student's name on the board
Call student to your desk
Scold
Refer student to posted rules
Remind student of earlier agreement
Say "Sh"
Call student's name
Threaten loss of recess
Inform of later conference
Threaten trip to office
Threaten call to parent
Change instructional activity
Take student outside to confer
Take away privileges or jobs
Provide adjustment time: exercise, drink, etc.
Have student place head on desk
Stand silently and wait for behavior change
Send to counselor
Move other catalytic students
Move student to front or rear
Move student to semi-isolation
Place student at desk outside door (check legality)
Send to the principal's office
Send to another teacher's room (need prior approval)

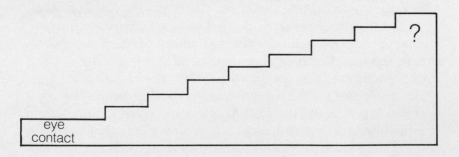

fort to the surrounding students. Kounin did find that the popularity and prestige of secondary teachers maximized the effectiveness of their desist techniques and students' work involvement, and therefore minimized misbehavior (Charles, 1981, pp. 48-49).

Seatwork assistance

Researchers have found that today's teachers allot an average of 40 to 62 percent of the class periods to independent study. If these findings are truly typical, then the most important teaching skills are possibly those associated with making appropriate assignments and concurrently assisting seatworkers. But the seatwork monitor must also enforce adherence to rules of conduct—rules which, when enforced, result in propitious study and research environments. Beyond a doubt, *effectively* managing a study period has not received enough attention.

Edmund Emmer et al. (1984, p. 98), in discussing seatwork, states that "if you notice commotion involving several students and you have no idea what is going on, this is a sign that you have not been monitoring closely enough." Emmer's statement emphasizes the need for teachers to move about the room and to remain alert to the total class. The antithesis of this attention is seatwork monitors who become sedentary, occupied with other tasks, or overly involved with a few students. Other initiatives associated with effectively managing seatworkers are the following:

1. Model the correct procedure and skills by doing the first couple of problems, questions, or tasks.
2. Post the assignment and due date.
3. Consider posting the necessary steps required for the assignment. For example: the steps involved in diagramming a sentence, the steps involved in writing a short poem (haiku), or the steps involved in dividing fractions.
4. Communicate study period rules. For example, may one student seek assistance from another? If so, under what conditions?
5. Remind the class that those signaling for assistance are to move ahead to the next part of their assignment or to read from their textbook until the teacher arrives. Another alternative is to provide students with weekly "quickie folders." The folders have

127

several short practice sheets, drill exercises, subject puzzles, or task sheets relating to the present unit of study. Some teachers give small bonuses for the successful completion of "quickies."

6. Help those students who are needing assistance, but do not only "chase hands." There is a need to check the progress of *all* students.

7. Communicate the signal system for students to use in requesting assistance. Remember that students with a waving hand and students who are passively waiting on the teacher's arrival are not on task and are not learning.

8. Remain aware that, while helping one student, the remaining class members may be behind you; you have thus lost your touch with the class. Consider implementing approaches such as seating students in shallow semicircles or, when necessary, have seated students stand up so that you can face the class, and pivot your body to continually maintain eye contact with all class members.

9. Collect and check work for evaluating students' progress to show the importance of seatwork and homework, and for compelling work completion.

10. Reinforce individual students by telling them that you appreciate good work habits.

11. Learn to show your appreciation to those who remain productive while waiting on your arrival: "Jim, thank you for continuing to work while waiting for me." (Remember the ripple effect discussed earlier.)

The greatest concern of many trainees is the fear that students will be disrespectful, will fight, or will ignore commands. Although these misbehaviors do sometime surface, the research of Frederic Jones finds that crisis events are infrequent. Instead, Jones finds that talking to neighbors makes up 80 percent of the misbehaviors and that most of the remaining 20 percent is in the form of unauthorized movement (Charles, 1983, p. 59). Knowing about these behavioral tendencies should be enough of a stimulus to make every teacher an *active* monitor during individualized seatwork, group work, and laboratory periods.

A survey conducted by Jones asked teachers how much time they, on the average, spent helping students who signaled for their assistance. Teachers thought they spent one to two minutes per visit, but, Jones said, "our stopwatches show[ed] that the average duration of such interactions [was] roughly four minutes" (Jones, 1979, p. 31). This meant that teachers were able to assist only six or seven students in twenty-five minutes of seatwork. It also meant that there was not enough remaining time to give attention and reinforcement to either the poorly motivated or the good workers. Under these conditions, there is a greater probability that students will get off task, get out of their chairs, and talk to neighbors. To lessen these probabilities, Jones recommends "Praise, Prompt, and Leave"—an assisting approach which limits each interaction to twenty to thirty seconds and, therefore provides up to seventy-five interactions during a twenty-five-minute study period.

The "Praise, Prompt, and Leave" approach requires teachers to perform two tasks per visit—in addition to leaving the student.

Step 1: Comment positively on some portion of the completed work: "Your heading is appropriately placed," "You've completed the first two steps," "You're on the right track," "You're on the correct page and ready to go," "Good job so far," etc.

Step 2: Give the child a prompt which allows him or her to take the next step with a high probability of success (Jones, 1979, p. 32). Examples of prompts are "That means . . .," "Look at the example on page 94," "Check to see if the decimal is in the correct place," and "Put the decimal here." Time is not used to focus on errors, nor to give answers, but to help the learner resume progress and advance one step at a time. The teacher quickly analyzes the students' work and instructs them what to do.

Step 3: Leave. Move quickly away from the student, leaving him to apply the teacher information. It is difficult for many teachers to leave without knowing that the student will correctly apply the information. But this approach gives the teacher time to return and give further assistance, provides more assistance to more learners, does not reinforce dependency, and discourages off-task behaviors.

Seatwork is a valuable opportunity for teachers to individualize instruction and for learners to conceptualize and apply the teacher's teachings. But seatwork also provides teachers with opportunities to show concern for student progress and to use

129

facial and verbal expressions in applauding good work and good behavior. These assisting and reinforcing acts indirectly communicate to students that a businesslike, academically focused teacher is also a friendly, warm, helpful, and caring person.

Questions and Tasks

1. Do you recall a teacher who consistently communicated with his or her eyes? How is eye communication more efficient than verbal communication?
   Analyzing yourself, which body expression will you need to modify in your attempt to show an emotion?

2. Why is it better to "swallow some pride" than to have a physical encounter?
   Describe an instance in which, as a teacher, you may stoically tell a student, "We'll take this matter up at a later time."

3. When you are very angry, what is the distance of your "life space"?
   Why should a teacher usually not attempt to stop an enraged student from leaving?

4. Why does society allow coaches to pat their players on the buttocks and older female teachers to hug students, but often frowns when male teachers fondly touch students?

5. Explain your reaction to the following statement: "Teachers who frequently use sarcasm, criticism, and roughness are usually ineffective classroom managers."

6. Do you predict yourself to be a low- or high-profile teacher? Which would you rather be? Why?

7. What are the characteristics of a good classroom rule? Why should teachers limit their rules to five?

8. Identify and describe one of your previous teachers who used a large amount of praise in managing students' behavior.
   Describe one of your former teachers who frequently used either punishment or fear in managing behavior.
   Although consequences should be administered, when pos-

sible, immediately after the rule is broken, what would be a situation in which the consequence should be delayed?

9. What is an advantage to a teacher or school using hierarchical consequences?

10. Mass punishment has been known to bring about compliance. Does this justify its usage? Explain your answer.

11. List three things that teachers should do to insure smooth transitions.
    What are the odds of a teacher who has trouble conducting transitions being an efficient teacher? Explain your answer.

12. Develop a list of increasingly severe desists by listing the desists on the stair steps.

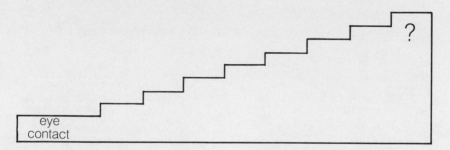

13. What is the "ripple effect" in classroom management?
    What did Jacob Kounin's research reveal about desists?

14. Why does the author say that teaching skills relating to seatwork may be more important than skills relating to large group instruction?

15. Reread the procedures associated with effectively managing seatworkers. Which five, in your opinion, are most important?

16. What are three advantages of Jones's "Praise, Prompt, and Leave" approach?

7

Special Managerial Concerns, Methods, and Resources

Even the most successful teachers periodically find themselves confronted with special managerial problems such as students wronging each other, physiological irregularities, frightened youngsters, sassing, and excuse making. Indeed, teachers are confronted with an array of problems unique to no other professional group as they simultaneously "wear the hats" of instructor, classroom manager, counselor, confidant, and temporary parent.

Controlling bodily functions

Students at times may be unable to control their bodily functions and emotions. Younger children, especially during the first week of school, sometimes accidentally wet their pants. This occurrence can be largely prevented by teachers scheduling regular restroom breaks and reminding the very young to take advantage of the opportunity. When a wetting does occur, first realize the embarrassment to the child, then see that the area is cleaned and the child moved to the office where a change of clothes can be sought. Later, privately discuss the incident with the child with the intent of determining whether the child was afraid or embarrassed to ask permission to be excused, was embarrassed to earlier use the restroom in front of his or her peers, or had other reasons for letting the accident occur. Assure the child that mistakes can happen, and cooperatively develop a plan to prevent future incidents. You might rehearse again the procedures for restroom breaks, reemphasize the importance of using the break for its intended purpose, and possibly provide special procedures—for example, allow the child to be the last in line if her or she is reluctant to be exposed in front of other children. In some serious cases it becomes necessary to keep a change of clothes at school.

Crying

Although there is no evidence supporting the notion that crying is harmful to children (Sloane, 1976, p. 53), it is harmful to a teacher's instructional efforts when a child cries at the slightest provocation. Not only is the crying student not on task, but the behavior disrupts the rest of the class. Students who frequently cry may be insecure, have a poor self-concept, feel unloved, or feel deprived, and this attitude and behavior may be reinforced by the attention they gain from crying. Indeed, most adults are sympathetic to a crying child and will seek to learn the cause, make the child feel more secure, and bolster the child's self-image. Teachers must remain alert to not become reinforcing agents to students who cry and have tantrums.

Some teachers of teachers recommend ignoring the crying child, if he or she is obviously not in pain, and waiting until the child acts in a relatively acceptable manner. When this state is reached, reinforce the improved behavior by complimenting the child on the ability to gain control and carry on the work (Sloane, 1976, pp. 53-59). Carolyn Evertson and her associates at the Research Center at the University of Texas (1981, pp. 94-95) recommend giving the child permission to cry but also recommend asking for a "temporary pause long enough for telling you the problem." In becoming engaged in the conversation, the child often does not resume crying. Should the crying continue, inform the child that it is alright to cry quietly and, when finished, to clean his or her face, get a drink, and rejoin the class activity. Naturally, extended crying cannot be allowed to disrupt instruction, and the child may need to be accompanied to the counselor or office. Do not reinforce crying by excessive attention and sympathy.

Fighting and aggressive behavior

Teachers infrequently must decide whether to directly intervene in a fight, to ignore it, or to seek assistance in stopping the altercation. For the youths protection, the situation cannot be ignored. The more difficult decision for you is whether you have the necessary influence and physical presence to separate the combatants without injuring and embarrassing yourself. After a crowd gathers it is extremely difficult to break up a fight; in this case, seek assistance from other teachers and the office.

Occasionally a class may have a bully who takes advantage of others by bossing, pushing, and hitting. There are also instances when normally well-behaved youngsters will playfully slap or shove another student. Teachers should quickly and consistently inform these aggressive students that this behavior is unacceptable and give no more than one warning before imposing a suitable consequence (Emmer et al., 1984, p. 105).

Rudeness toward the teacher

Unquestionable rudeness and defiance toward teachers comes under the "severe clause" of most anyone's management model, but teachers must be cautious to avoid overreacting. There are instances when students truthfully do not realize the offensive nature of their statements. However, when the rudeness is obvious or repeated, the student should be confronted—but not through the use of a "power struggle" approach. Power struggles with students are not appropriate school entertainment for the class. Rather, pointedly inform the student that the comment is not appreciated, but that rather than cause a further interruption of the lesson, you will be discussing it together shortly. This gives the student and you a chance to "cool down," keeps the student from disrupting the class, and allows you to complete the lesson. Later, when discussing the incident with the student, remember not to argue, give the student a chance to tell his or her point of view, and provide the disruptful youngster with a reasonable consequence and a plan for preventing future incidents of this sort. The defensiveness of rule violators is often lessened by starting the conference with a calmly asked question similar to "What was it that I did to cause your disrespectful statement or act?" It is disarming to defensive students when the authority figure wants to solve the problem rather than blame and punish the offender.

Occasionally a student may disregard a teacher's order to curb his or her remarks or to leave the room and report to the school's disciplinarian. Should this situation arise, it will be necessary to send another student to the office for assistance.

Tattling

Like wetting, tattling occurs primarily in lower-grade classrooms for various reasons, including competitiveness, egocentricity, jealousy, and attention getting. Although tempting, a teacher should not refuse to listen, because sometimes the informant offers information that is important to the maintenance of safety and fairness. Unfortunately, the teacher's attention can reinforce the chronic tattle-tale. Johanna Lemlech (1979, p. 38) advocates the use of teacher responses similar to "Why are you concerned?" "Why are you letting me know about this?" and "Is it your problem?" when the information is judged to be unimportant to the students' welfare. These responses are designed to help the informant analyze himself or herself.

Another approach is to announce that each student should attempt to resolve any complaints with the responsible person. If this does not take care of the problem, then the plaintiff may write the complaint on a slip of paper and place it in a "complaint box." The slips are not to be signed. The teacher reads the complaints at the end of the day while asking the class if each is important or should be disregarded. This procedure is most helpful when a rash of complaints surface. The procedure will usually significantly retard tattle-tales because it takes more effort and thought to write a complaint than to verbally express one.

Squabbles

Some teachers spend considerable time acting as negotiators and referees in settling student squabbles. Kathy Hummel's (1981, p. 32) technique, however, requires minimum time and also serves to inhibit those children who squabble:

1. Bring all "combatants" together.
2. Say, "You seem to be having a problem."
3. Optional step: Say, "Tell me about it" or omit the statement and proceed to Step #4.

4. Say, "I would like to see you settle this so you may go on playing or working as friends. Sit down here and talk about what you can do to settle the problem and be friends."
5. See that all squabbling parties sit down. Sitting seems to have a cooling affect on upset individuals.
6. Say, "Be sure to come and tell me what you decide about how you can be friends."
7. If there is an item (ball, pencil, etc.) involved, say, "I'll hold this until you have it settled."
8. Turn your back on, or move away from, the discussion. Usually within 60 seconds the parties will inform you of their agreement.
9. After hearing the terms, ask, "Is everyone satisfied with this?" If the answer is "no," repeat steps #4 through #9.
10. If the answer is "yes," the children shake hands on the deal.

Should the above technique not work, it may be necessary to become a mediator. But it nearly always works, and, again, it has served as a squabble preventative. As Kathy Hummel says, "I've witnessed students bound toward me with tattles on the tips of their tongues and then veer off course saying, 'She'll just make us sit down and talk about it—let's go play.' "

Excuses

There is a big difference between people who "try." Some put forth considerable effort and attention, while others say they try but make little, if any, effort. Individuals composing the second group sometimes actually believe themselves to be incapable of success, especially when others repeatedly accept their excuses: "I'll try to be on time," "I'll try to complete it," and "I tried to do it." What is there to motivate a change in behavior if the person's excuse is accepted? Curwin and Mendler say that individuals who preface their promises and excuses with "I'll try" or "I tried" usually have little intention of achieving.

After all, how can anybody make demands from cute little Mary who does nothing but tries every time; or pudgy Sammy who tries not to eat four Devil Dogs every afternoon but eats them anyway; or poor Tommy who has been trying not to push other kids around for years but keeps pushing them? (Curwin and Mendler, 1980, p. 229)

Robert Martin (1981, pp. 84-85), who believes teachers should discourage excuses and make student excuses "ineffective as a way of avoiding the consequences for their actions," has identified six common forms of excuses.

1. Denial: "I didn't do it."
2. Blaming others: "It's her fault."
3. Blaming circumstances: "The glass fell off the table."
4. Blaming authority: "But that's what I was told to do."
5. Personal idiosyncrasies: "I've always been late."
6. Self-reproach: "I guess I'm just lazy."

Teachers gain nothing by asking misbehavers "why" they did or did not do something. Seldom do they know why they misbehaved, and such a question encourages the formulation of an excuse. Furthermore, teachers should not accept a student's "good intention," nor any of the other above forms of excuses, as justification for the behavior. Good intentions are usually poor substitutes for action. Martin believes that students who truly intend to change their behavior should be willing to come up with a specific plan of action to alter their behavior—they should make a commitment. A concrete plan promotes a greater chance of success than does a general promise that "I'll try."

William Glasser has the following problem-solving approach for dealing with a barrage of excuses from individuals involved in an incident (Martin, 1981, p. 85).

1. Ask everyone involved in the incident to state exactly what he or she did. (You are not asking for reasons, excuses, or justification; you are simply asking for a statement of what happened.)
2. Pose the question without pinning the blame and without being judgmental. ("Janet, what did you do?")
3. If a student tries to sidestep your question by pointing at others, simply listen politely and then ask, "What did you do?"
4. When excuses are offered, ask, "What could you do to make sure that this situation doesn't happen again?" or "What can you do to solve the problem?" (These responses neither affirm nor deny the validity of an excuse—they place the responsibility for the behavior back on the student.)

Corporal punishment

Corporal punishment is disciplinary action through the use of physical force. In general, the laws of most states allow teachers and administrators to "correct" student conduct by the use of reasonable force, force which is necessary under the circumstances. In fact, corporal punishment is illegal only in Massachusetts, New Jersey, Maine, Hawaii, and some local school districts (Kaercher, 1984, p. 137). Although most teachers are granted the privilege of using corporal punishment, few efficient teachers use physical force in today's classrooms. Most modern-day teachers wish to retain the privilege but abhor the actual use of physical force to regulate students' behavior.

Individuals who are knowledgeable about school law and classroom management techniques warn teachers to use corporal punishment only as a last resort for at least four reasons:

1. Physical force, as a method of producing desirable behavior, usually produces only a temporary improvement.
2. There are less barbarous techniques to use than physical force.
3. The teacher who uses physical force has apparently reached the end of the "desist rope." He or she will probably impose an additional amount of force on repeated offenders.
4. Users of corporal punishment have opened themselves up to charges of battery.

For battery to occur, the teacher must make contact with the complaining individual. The contact does not need to be with the person's body: it may be with what the person is wearing or carrying. If a teacher rips a boy's shirt off his back, a battery has occurred. Another requirement in proving battery is that the contact is made in a rude or angry manner (Gatti and Gatti, 1975, p. 36). Knowing these characteristics of battery, one can easily see how an upset teacher who uses physical force could end up being lawfully charged with battery of a student.

Those few educators who insist on using corporal punishment must administer it under the following guidelines (Gatti and Gatti, 1975, p. 90):

1. The punishment must be reasonable and necessary.
2. The state law, district and school policies must allow corporal punishment.
3. The student must know why he or she is being punished.
4. The student must have had an opportunity to explain his or her side of the story leading up to the punishment.
5. The punishment should not be excessive and should be consistent with the student's age and sex.
6. It should be administered in the presence of a witness.
7. It should not be administered by an angry or emotionally upset person.

The teaching profession of this day has a wealth of psychological and pedagogical research and knowledge at its disposal—enough to make the use of physical punishment an antiquated disciplinary approach. There is virtually never a justifiable reason for today's teachers to employ the consequential floggings of the Horace Mann era. Mann, an advocate of public-supported schooling, reported that an average of sixty-five floggings were administered each day in a school of 250 students. This abundant use of floggings in the 1800s was the natural result of the rules and consequences as outlined for a teacher in 1848 (Wallen and Wallen, 1978, p. 3):

Rules	Lashes
Boys and girls fighting together	4
Quarreling	4
Fighting	5
Gameleing or beting	4
Tellying lyes	7
Nich naming each other	4
Swaring	8

Stealing and cheating

Thievery and cheating are possibly the most difficult behaviors that teachers periodically encounter. Both are touchy character problems. Dishonesty is not ethnocentric, nor is it associated with any specific socioeconomic group. It is found in the wealthy, the poor, the educated, and the uneducated. Especially because dishonesty is a character problem, teachers and parents should be more concerned with correcting the child's character than with punishing his or her body or mind.

Parents and guardians sometimes indirectly teach children to be dishonest. They may instruct the child to tell door-to-door sales-persons that they are not at home, or to tell a caller that they are indisposed. Parents may also teach dishonesty by directing their children to tell ticket sellers that they are younger than they actually are so they can pay less admission. Children also see role models smuggling purchases through customs and bringing unpurchased supplies home from the office. We, and our children, are born neither with innate honesty nor dishonesty. Values are taught and learned.

Stealing

A child, deprived of items he or she considers basic to his or her well-being, may practice an attitude that stealing is an expeditious way to acquire items belonging to another person. Another child, for a less basic reason, may steal to gain attention from either a parent or a teacher. Thefts also occur when a vengeful person retaliates against the "enemy" by taking his or her belongings. Some youths steal because of challenges from peers—in this case stealing is a way to be accepted. Others enjoy the excitement and challenge of the act and its results. Another underlying cause is that many children's tangible wishes were immediately satisfied when they were very young and they were never taught that individuals must sometimes do without (Dreikurs, Grunwald, and Pepper, 1982, pp. 211-214, 257-267).

Since such a large number of burglaries go unsolved in our society, even though investigated by trained personnel, teachers are not expected to solve all acts of dishonesty. But once it is ascertained that a missing item was not misplaced or lost, teachers are obliged to try to help the victim recover the property, to identify the misbehaver, and to help the misbehaver find more ethical behavioral alternatives. Regrettably, the teacher can do little more than describe what is missing, acknowledge to the class that it seems to have been taken—not misplaced or lost—and then provide a situation that will allow a confidential return of the item. A call to the victim's parents will be appreciated and sometimes will reveal additional evidence. Again, these efforts should be made only after the victim has thoroughly searched for the item. Frequently items are not stolen as suspected, but instead have been lost or misplaced. Children will sometimes swear they remember wearing the item during the previous thirty minutes only to later find it at home.

If a student, *beyond any reasonable doubt*, is identified as the thief, he or she should privately be confronted and asked to return the item or make restitution. Teachers should recall the earlier reasons for children taking others' property and attempt to determine the reason behind the student's act. If the underlying cause becomes apparent (attention, revenge, modeling, challenge, immaturity towards gratification, satisfying basic physical needs such as food), then the teacher should employ counseling techniques to help the child determine and choose more acceptable behaviors.

Teachers must heed three concluding warnings when handling situations involving stolen property.

1. Never, never accuse a student of dishonesty unless he or she is guilty beyond a doubt. Unjustly accusing someone of dishonesty attacks that person's self-concept, his or her most prized possession. To be falsely accused has a profound effect on both the accused and his or her relationship with the accuser.
2. Because it is difficult to solve problems involving missing property, it is tempting for teachers to assume that everyone is guilty until proven innocent. For example, a teacher might have all students stand against the wall to be searched. Do not use such approaches.
3. Do not, in frustration, use mass punishment. Do not punish the entire class for the misdeed of one or a few; punish only the misbehaver. Do not attempt to force the guilty to come forward by giving continuing punishment to the class.

Cheating

The motivation behind cheating in the classroom is not to learn the copied material but to avoid tangible evidence of failure, to avoid punishing reactions from parents and teachers, or to receive the reinforcement which accompanies successful grades. Although these motivational flaws appear to be solely linked to the cheater, such is often not the case. Cheating will seldom occur when a learner is appropriately placed at his or her learning level with a good reinforcing teacher. But schools' systems of placing students by chronological age is detrimental to appropriate placement because grouping by age results in many students being expected to work at an inappropriate achievement level. In this situation, cheating will frequently surface. One who is sensitive towards the unreasonableness of expecting students to achieve at levels beyond their capabilities may be tempted to overlook a youngster who cheated on an assignment or test beyond his skill level. The rationale underlying such leniency is that this cheating is not as amoral as when a youth cheats only because of laziness—although both are dishonest acts and should not be disregarded. Someday our schools may implement continuous progress or non-graded curricula so that students of the same chronological ages are not erroneously recognized as academic equals and "emphasis is placed on what is learned rather than on getting a good grade" (Sloane, 1976, p. 123).

Procedural guidelines for seatwork, homework, special projects, and testing should all be discussed during the orientation days and repeated thereafter. The discussion should include an overview of expectations and the resulting consequences, and should also cover rules regarding cheating. Thereafter, it is to be hoped, cheating will be infrequent or nonexistent because the class members will be practicing their own value systems. If a student does not practice honesty, then the teacher is obligated to insist on compliance by both preventive and corrective measures.

Seatwork and Homework. In planning assignments, teachers must determine whether the work is to be completed individually, in pairs, or in larger groups. Different instructional and work procedures necessitate different rules of conduct. Students required to work individually will usually do so when the teacher is in touch with the situation and actively monitors the work session. But insuring individually completed homework is another matter. When evaluating students' papers, teachers periodically see an unbelievable similarity between the work of two or more students. Teachers in this situation will often inform the two children of this close similarity without accusing them of cheating: "Jack, I saw a phenomenal thing. I noticed that you and Bill used the exact same quotes and resources. Accidents do happen." This type of statement can serve as a notification of your perceptiveness and as a warning, or the teacher may wish to pursue the incident by asking them—in private—how they think such an accident could occur. *Remember:* a teacher should not accuse a student of a dishonest act without being absolutely certain that he or she is right because the accusation is so onerous that it may be remembered forever. One method of discouraging cheating on projects and homework, and for investigating whether students have done their own work, is to include an evaluative interview as part of the grading. This periodic practice tends to discourage future cheating by informing students that their scores on written work and projects must be compatible with their knowledge offered in the evaluative interviews.

Experienced teachers often develop a perceptiveness in knowing who is taking dishonest shortcuts. This alertness is developed by acquiring a thorough knowledge of the subject area and materials, by evaluating all work assignments, by periodically discussing students' work progress with them, and by remembering and keeping work of previous students. The following measures are also helpful in preventing cheating on homework.

1. Announce during orientation the consequences for cheating. Remaining after school to redo the work, conference with parents, and a test grade based on only the portion completed prior to the incident are examples.
2. The use of two different assignments of equivalent difficulty can help prevent copying.
3. Make certain that each student is capable of doing the homework.
4. Do the first part of the assignment, modeling the correct procedure and skills.

Tests. Cheating during tests is often done with varying degrees of crudeness and creativity. Crudeness is evident when a student openly and obviously continues to look at another student's paper. This is not the same as unconsciously—and unintentionally—looking at a neighbor's work. Others may write information on cuffs, legs, hands, paper slips, or a desk's surface before the test.

These approaches can be discouraged by announcing that all materials except a pencil are to be under (or in) the desks and all surfaces are to be clean. Inform the class that you will *hand* each person a test *upside down* and that it is to remain so until they are instructed otherwise. When each one has a test, inform the class that no one is to start answering questions at this time—just to listen. Then instruct them to turn the test over and put their names in the upper corner, and inform them of corrections, deletions, and additions. This procedure insures their attention, eliminates multiple explanations of directions, and also allows the proctor to examine each student's desk surface. Additional measures to insure honesty during testing are as follows:

1. Take precautions to insure that the test questions and test copies are not seen before the test is administered.
2. Actively monitor at all times during the testing.
3. Do not leave the room, or become engaged in clerical tasks, and do not discuss items with early finishers.
4. Consider the use of different forms of a test to make potential copiers ineffectual.
5. Spread chairs far apart.

If a student should continue to copy even when the teacher actively monitors, the teacher may wish to give a blank sheet of paper to the person who is being copied with the instructions to please use the page as a cover sheet. Although this approach does not accuse the copier, he or she gets the message and becomes ineffectual in the dishonesty, and the desist is disruptive to only one student.

Isolation

A teacher may occasionally find it necessary to isolate a student who is unwilling (or unable) to abide by the classroom rules. Although isolation or time-out areas are sometimes established outside the classrooms, most isolations are handled within. Dewey and Judith Carducci (1984, p. 65) believe that the areas should be recognizable as "discrete areas" that are used as a "preferable alternative to removing a disruptive student from the room." A

145

discrete area may be a chair in the rear corner of the room or an area partially separated from the class membership by a filing cabinet or screen. The area should be devoid of visual and aural stimuli, in eye contact with the teacher, safe, not readily in view of other students, and away from traffic, doors, and windows.

Classroom managers must not only plan the physical arrangement of the isolation area, but they must also determine the reason (purpose) for developing the area, what behavior is expected of the student while in isolation, and the duration of the time-out. Teachers view isolation differently: some use it solely for punishment, some as a period for the child to "cool off"—to gain some self-control—and others see it as time for the student to analyze his or her behavior, to consider more desirable (alternative) behavior, and to synthesize a commitment to behave more appropriately. The teacher's purpose for isolating may influence what is to be expected of the child while in isolation: that is, a teacher may want the misbehaver to face away from the class, to do seatwork, to not do seatwork, or to do nothing except think about his or her behavior.

The purpose behind the isolation may also influence its duration. Teachers who use it as punishment may dictate a set duration of five minutes or until the child has quieted. In contrast, a teacher who seeks a commitment from a student may direct the student to remain in isolation until he or she agrees to a plan for improved behavior.

Some schools have out-of-room detention or holding areas. These supervised areas are a resource for teachers who are unable to control the behavior of disruptive or uncooperative students—teachers who have reached a point where they must tell the misbehaver, "If you can't control yourself, I'm going to control you *for* you until you can" (Carducci and Carducci, 1984, p. 69). Out-of-room holding areas may be nothing more than a chair in the office, a chair in a cooperating teacher's room, a chair in the hall, or a room with an aid or teacher for supervising students temporarily expelled from classrooms. Although schools differ, supervisors of holding rooms are usually instructed to do the following:

Initially encourage seatwork
Not tutor (although some allow supervisors to assist)
Not visit with students nor allow them to visit with each other
Not listen to excuses but to simply inform students that they must

deal with their teacher

Regulate the students' departures and destinations

School policies sometimes permit teachers to isolate students in the hallways, but unless the procedure is expressly an administrative policy, it is not recommended. Students who cannot be seen are not properly supervised, and improperly supervised students periodically have accidents. Knowing this, one can anticipate a charge of negligence if a student is injured while being improperly supervised. The office is one of the poorest isolation areas, and its usage as such indicates that the school's decision makers often "do not understand the concept of time-out" (Walker and Shea, 1984, pp. 105-106). Time-out is not to be a stimulating and reinforcing experience where misbehavers are allowed to view irate parents, listen to office gossip, staple papers, and run errands. Rather, when the office is used as a time-out area, it should have the same characteristics recommended for an isolation space in a special room.

Cultural differences

America, and therefore its communities and institutions, has been described by some as a "melting pot." This ideology, which was popularized by Israel Zangwell, encouraged immigrants to abandon their cultural and ethical customs and to be fused into a new emerging common culture—primarily with Anglo cultural characteristics (Banks, 1974). This ideology of "changing for the good of the whole" has had meritorious effects but has not been totally successful—nor should it be. It is healthy for groups to retain some of their cultural diversities as long as they have a commitment to the core values of justice, equality, and human dignity.

Our classrooms are often pots of mixed cultures containing racial, religious, and social groups with different beliefs and traits. Not only are classrooms composed of different cultural groups with differing belief systems and customs, but members of the various cultural groups frequently splinter into subcultures with differing beliefs and values. This sociological phenomenon adds an additional managerial dimension to teachers' roles. Teachers should not only remain respectful of their students' cultural beliefs and customs and foster multicultural education, but they need to also incorporate this knowledge into their interactions to avoid multicultural conflicts. To do less will increase the likelihood of unnecessary confrontations.

The following are examples of behaviors associated with different groups (Zintz, 1969; Charles, 1981; Lightfoot, 1978; Banks, 1974).

Hispanics enjoy togetherness and well-being within the group, whereas Anglos are more likely to prize being first or being best.

Hispanics and Indians are oriented toward the present rather than the future. Punctuality is not of major importance, and why save for a rainy day? Be generous and it will come back to you.

Indians see success as being a good person within the group. Anglos are more concerned with their individual success.

Mexican Americans are very sensitive to both praise and criticism from teachers.

Chicano and Indian children should not be expected to look adults in the eye.

Yaqui Indian youth should not be expected to perform before they are well prepared. If a task cannot be done well, they feel there is little need to engage in the activity.

How ignorance of cultural traits can cause classroom confrontations is illustrated by a story (touched upon earlier) which was told to the author by a teacher of Eskimo (Indian) children. The young teacher recounted that while he was scolding a youngster for not doing his work, the student continually stared at his desk. The Anglo teacher shouted, "Look me in the eye when I'm speaking to you." But the student continued to ignore the commands. The teacher related that he "cooled down" somewhat and told the boy to see him after school. Later during the day, while venting his frustration to an experienced teacher, he learned that the eye contact he was demanding was a disrespectful act in the child's culture. Such incidents, and an increasing realization that our schools are in themselves a culturally diverse society, have caused many states to mandate the inclusion of multicultural education into their teacher-training programs.

As educators we must respect the belief systems of cultural groups other than our own. We need to remain cognizant that there is no one best life style and that all cultural groups, races, religions, and socioeconomic groups are equally legitimate under the laws of this nation. This does not mean that an individual with different values, from any one of the over three hundred ethnic groups in this country, should be excused when he or she violates reasonable rules and laws. Yet again, what is a "reasonable" requirement to a teacher or school may be prohibited by the religious beliefs of a child. This statement reinforces Raths's belief (see Chapter 2, "Values and Morality") that discipline problems frequently result when the child's values are different from the values of the teacher or school. When these situations arise, the child is caught wanting to participate in the class's activities but also wanting to be loyal to the beliefs and customs of his or her cultural group.

Jehovah's Witnesses children who attend public schools typify students with values and customs that are significantly different from those of their schools. These children are taught to show respect and obedience toward their country's laws but believe the flag salute to be worship and say, "We cannot conscientiously give what we view as worship to anyone or anything except our God" (Watchtower, 1983, p. 13). This right to refrain from pledging allegiance to the flag was upheald by the United Supreme Court in 1943 (West Virginia State Board of Education v. Barnette, 319 U.S. 624 (1943)) (Data Research, 1987, p. 154, 486). Jehovah's Witnesses also view the national anthem as a hymn or prayer set to music and do not rise when it is played. If they are already standing when the anthem starts, it is not necessary for them to be seated. In addition, educators should not expect Witnesses to sing school songs or participate in organized sports, participate in school politics, celebrate an individual's birthday, nor observe Christmas, Easter, and other holidays commonly celebrated in the public schools.

Human resources

Even the most successful teacher may encounter problems ranging from cultural confrontations and child neglect to deviancy and destruction of property. No teacher is always successful. This is to be expected in view of the fact that an elementary teacher works with approximately 300 different children during a ten-year span, and a secondary teacher may easily be responsible for the actions of 1,500 students during a ten-year stretch. It must also be remembered that our nation attempts to keep all children in school—regardless of their interests, respect for authority, different priorities or needs, and varying achievement levels. Under these conditions, incorrigible relations are destined to periodically appear in any teacher's classroom.

In circumstances involving teacher-student conflicts, teachers should not turn to last-resort measures, especially such a measure as physical force, until they have exhausted the many managerial systems, methods, and skills advocated throughout these pages. In addition to the vast variety of managerial techniques, there are also the following human resources available for assisting teachers in changing students' behavior.

Counselors. School counselors can provide and interpret students' psychological and achievement test results and their personal history, and will frequently know of problems underlying deviant behavior. Counselors are also good third parties for sharing and releasing your managerial frustrations.

Psychologists. School psychologists are available in many districts for administering and interpreting psychological and educational tests, and for the diagnoses and therapeutics of problem cases. They diagnose and offer therapeutics for the retarded child, the superior child doing inferior work, students with special ability, and the child with deviant behavior. Larger school districts usually have staff psychologists, and smaller districts frequently form "cooperatives" in which two or more districts use the services of one or more psychologists.

Principals and Assistant Principals. There are vast differences in administrators' supervisory abilities as well as in teachers' instructional proficiencies. Some principals are capable of observing, analyzing, and offering helpful instructional and managerial suggestions. Regardless of a principal's supervisory capabilities, however, troubled teachers should recognize their principals as colleagues that should be kept informed when teacher-student encounters develop.

Teaching Colleagues. In each building there are respected, efficient teachers who will work with colleagues in helping solve managerial and behavioral problems.

College Personnel. Classroom teachers should not hesitate to request teacher trainers to help them correct the behaviors of students.

Mental Health Centers. It has been estimated that 10 percent of all school-age children suffer from behavioral or emotional disorders—disorders which may be caused by complex interactions of genetic preconditions and environmental variables. Referrals to centers are not made directly by teachers, but usually by district administrators, family services, state departments of mental health, or through private family placement. Centers offer out-patient services that give youth the opportunity to work with a therapist on a scheduled basis. Residential services are available for youth whose behavior, environment, or associations may be interfering with the ability to follow the rules of society.

School Social Worker. Although in most schools all referrals to the school social worker go through the principal, teachers should recognize the role of the social worker in today's schools. Much of today's social workers' time is used in initiating and conducting P.L. 94-142 meetings, during which individualized education programs (IEP) are developed, reviewed, and revised for handicapped children. However, social workers are also available to help other referred children learn and grow as worthy citizens. The social worker is often involved in assessing the child's home life, school life, and other influences which contribute to a child's problems.

School Nurse. Although it is not his or her primary role, the school nurse may serve periodically as a consultant in matters relating to students' achievement and misbehavior. Obviously, the nurse should be contacted if a child is suspected of having a visual or auditory loss that may affect the student's attentiveness. Likewise, the nurse can advise teachers regarding such ailments as diabetes, seizures, hygiene, sexual concerns, and behaviors brought on by drug intake.

Supervisors and Department Heads. Some supervisory personnel have been excellent teachers and therefore may be able to help correct a behavioral or managerial problem. When these personnel are unable to assist the classroom teacher, they are often in a position to bring in a consultant.

Parents. There are exceptions, but parents want their children to achieve academically, be well mannered, and respect and be respected by their teachers. Because of this attitude—plus the fact that parents and guardians hold powerful reinforcers in the form of free play and time, allowances, TV rights, car keys, sweets, dating privileges, and telephone privileges—parents and teachers can be great allies and will find little need to regulate youth's behavior through the use of physical force. Most inappropriate behavior will improve when a youth's parents and teacher develop, implement, and consistently enforce a behavior contract stipulating the required behavior and resulting consequences. Naturally, there must be continual (at least weekly) communication between the allies.

These human resources are potential consultants that can be drawn upon to assist you in better understanding your students and in solving both *their* problems—and *your* problems. These resources and the other teachings of this book are akin to a buried energy source. Untapped and unused this book's research findings, management models, and knowledge of the skills and methods of effective teachers will result in no change to you or to your profession. To change and to grow in teaching effectiveness require the giving up of beliefs and practices—a willingness to not only unlearn and learn but also to practice one's professional teachings. Hopefully you have conceptualized the teachings of *Becoming An Effective Classroom Manager* and have placed it into your knowledge bank ready for retrieval. But let's remember Madeline Hunter's wisdom that "Learning is like money in the bank; it is great to have it there but it's only useful when you pull it out and use it" (Brandt, 1985, p. 62).

Questions and Tasks

1. The author once found his student teacher to be very upset. The cooperating teacher was attempting to correct the wetting habit of a first grader by placing a "pamper" over the child's damp jeans. The child wore the diaper the remainder of the day. Evaluate the approach.

2. What is your opinion of the procedure advocated by Carolyn Evertson and her associates for handling crying?

3. When should a teacher physically intervene in a fight? When should a teacher not intervene?

4. Evaluate the appropriateness of a teacher physically removing a rude student.

5. Evaluate Lemlech's procedure for dealing with tattlers.
Can you give tattlers too much attention? Explain.
Should you ignore all student complaints?

6. Would Kathy Hummel's method be appropriate for dealing with a squabble between high school students? Justify your answer.

7. Why are good intentions poor excuses?
Could Glasser's procedure be appropriately used with high school students involved in a squabble?

8. Are there recommendations that should be added to or deleted from Gatti and Gatti's guidelines for administering corporal punishment? Explain your answer.

9. Can you recall an incident in which you modeled dishonesty to a younger person?
It is difficult to find methods for handling stealing. Do you have any suggestions, apart from those given here?
Can you recall an incident in which you were falsely accused of a dishonest act? If so, is it still vivid in your mind? Why?

10. Think of and describe an additional example in which a teacher may make an error in judgment if he or she does not know a student's cultural customs and beliefs.

11. Review the "human resources" available for assisting teachers in changing students' behavior. Which four will you probably use most frequently?

Part IV

Appendices

Appendix A

Time Expenditures: Lunch Count and Dismissal

Sometimes benevolent, caring programs and procedures, which are imposed by societal and administrative requirements, produce situations that are handicapping and stressful to classroom teachers. This point is well illustrated by a student teacher's frustrations in being required to act as an accountant for meals and being required to build her instructional program around the convenience of others:

It is 8:15, the bell rings, and students begin to enter the classroom. With lesson plans in hand you are prepared to begin a productive morning of learning. Right? Wrong?

At 8:15 students are allowed to enter the classroom; however, by 8:25 those eating breakfast have left again. In the meantime the lunch count (and breakfast count *and* extra milk count) begins. Juggling full-price lunches, reduced-price lunches, free lunches, charges, breakfast money, and charged meals is no small task. This is made especially difficult when breakfast eaters are filing back in one at a time, stopping by the desk to say something on the long journey to their seats. And of course there is always at least one tardy, which means changing lunch count totals, office slips, and books.

At 8:45 all of those eating breakfast are back. Ready to begin? No! Now remedial reading students leave for their class. In all this confusion, besides the lunch count and attendance being taken, daily chores are done, and a bathroom trip takes place.

At 9:00 it is time to switch classes for reading groups. It is finally time to get busy. But remember, remedial reading students are not back until 9:20-9:30. Unless review takes place at this time, the entire lesson must be taught again and assignments given over for the few who have returned by 9:30.

At last 9:30 is here! Everyone is in class. No one is missing. Just think, a full thirty minutes of teaching can take place before the 10:00 recess!

Mrs. Debbie Bottom
Student Teacher
Grade 3

With more thought, the administration of this school district could have scheduled pull-outs (for remedial classes) to coincide with a time when the same subject was being taught by the classroom teacher. Although it is not simple to make remedial teachers' schedules compatible with the schedules of several other teachers, the problem could be eased by methods such as pulling the students out less frequently but for longer periods, and by having classroom teachers change the time when certain subjects are taught. For example, reading does not need to be taught during the morning hours—research does not support this mythical, sacred-cow practice (Dunn and Dunn, 1978, pp. 16, 396, 398).

Debbie Bottom's supervising teacher reveals how her former school handled lunch monies in a way that was less stressful for teachers and less wasteful of instructional time. She also discusses a better system for getting children on the bus at the end of the day:

The system of the teacher taking lunch money is a time-consuming task for the beginning of a day. I formerly worked in a system where the secretary was responsible for taking the money from the students. At the time the students paid, they were given a lunch ticket for that day. The students took the ticket to their room and placed the ticket in a pocket of a chart containing their name. The teacher spent no time handling money or figuring a lunch book of any kind. Then at lunch a student could hand out the lunch tickets. Those having no lunch ticket were those who had brought their lunch. Either the secretary or an aide was seated at the door of the lunchroom collecting the tickets for that day. This system was very efficient.

In the afternoon when the 3:20 bell rings, the students that ride early buses leave. The rest of the students remain in the room until an upper-grade student runs down the hall hollering the number of the bus that has arrived. Then all of the students on that bus run up the hall to go get on that bus. This procedure continues until all of the bus students are gone. The walkers are then permitted to go.

It would seem that a better system might be to let the walkers go when the 3:20 bell rings. Then after they are out of the room let the bus riders all go to the lunchroom. They could be organized by bus number. All students riding the same bus could be seated together; then when that bus arrives they could file out. This would save confusion and free the teacher from having to police the students for fifteen to twenty minutes. The teachers could be grading, running off papers, or getting ready for the next day.

Mrs. Marilyn Bryant
Supervising Teacher
Grade 3

Appendix B

"Funny money" Management System

Judy Mannhard, Student Teacher and
Tammy Zaccardelli, Supervising Teacher

Classroom management is an essential part of good teaching. An effective teacher should have a classroom management system that reinforces good behavior and weakens the undesirable behavior of the student. The following classroom management system is one that I have observed and also used in my third-grade student teaching experience. I have found it to be a very effective system in dealing with management in the classroom.

The system is set up in such a way that students are rewarded with play money for good behavior and good academic progress, while undesirable behavior is weakened by fines paid with play money. Each student is issued $100 in play money at the beginning of the school year, and the money is to be kept in his or her desk. The money is issued only in $5 and $10 bills, as shown in this example:

Since each student is issued $100 at the beginning of the year, the teacher will need to begin by printing a large sum of money. After the initial $100 is issued, no further money is issued except in the form of earnings.

The fines and earnings *posted* in the classroom are as follows:

Fines

$10.00

   1. Incomplete or late paper

$5.00

   2. Talking out or talking out during work time
   3. Disobeying school rules
   4. Not keeping busy at your seat
   5. Tattling over nothing
   6. Sloppy, messy work
   7. Messy desk and area
   8. Slowly lining up; talking in line
   9. Using bathroom without pass
  10. Not paying attention or following directions

Earnings

1.	"A" paper in grade book	$5.00
2.	Book report	$5.00
3.	Unusual, kind deed	$5.00/$10.00
4.	Completion of color in SRA	$5.00

*** $20 earned a week = 1 piece of candy of your choice

It is important that these rules are discussed with students so that they have a clear understanding of how the system works. The teacher must be consistent in issuing fines and earnings for the system to be effective. To issue a fine, the teacher merely states that the fine is due. An example would be "You owe me $5 for talking" or "That will be $5." It should be explained to students that if the misbehavior occurs during the time the teacher is giving the lesson, the student is to wait until the lesson is over to put the fine on the teacher's desk.

To keep track of earnings, each student is responsible for keeping a "money sheet" at his or her desk showing the earnings for the week. This is merely a sheet of notebook paper that the student brings to the teacher's desk when earnings are collected. For example, when a student earns $5 for a book report, he or she brings the money sheet to the teacher, who marks "$5 BR" on the sheet in red ink. Each Friday afternoon the teacher calls up students one or two at a time for their money sheets to be checked. As each money sheet is checked, the teacher draws a line under the last amount entered to show the end of that week. The next week's earnings are recorded under the teacher's last check point. If a student has earned $20 that week, he or she may choose a piece of candy from a candy jar that contains items such as suckers, hard candy, and Sweet Tarts. Those students who have not earned $20 that week should be given an encouraging word from the teacher to try a little harder next week. Only the money earned during that week will qualify a student to choose candy.

At the end of the first quarter of school, a "store" is set up in the classroom where students can spend the money they have earned from the beginning of the quarter. The store may be set up on a large table at the back of the classroom with items for sale that the teacher has collected. These items need not be expensive and may include such things as stickers, erasers, toy cars, pencils, toy rings and bracelets, and candy. The teacher may group the merchandise on the table with signs stating the price, for example, "Stickers— $10," "Bracelets—$50," or "Erasers—$40." The prices may seem high to the students, but they should be reminded that they were given $100 at the beginning of the year.

Before students begin shopping, the teacher instructs them to save back $30 in their desks with which to pay future fines. The remainder of their money may be used to spend at the store, or they may be allowed to save it, if they wish, and carry it over to the next quarter to spend at the next store. The students should write their names on a slip of paper and put the papers in a can; the teacher then draws the slips randomly out of the can to determine the order in which students will be allowed to shop. Groups of shoppers should be kept to three or four at a time. A time limit of five or ten minutes should be set for each group. There will occasionally be students who do not have any money left by the end of the quarter because they have paid fines. These students will be disappointed at not being able to shop and usually show a marked improvement in behavior the next quarter. If their money supply is completely depleted and they are assessed additional fines, they must make out IOUs to the teacher. These IOUs are paid by doing classroom chores. An example of such a chore would be to clean up around the classroom. These chores give the students an opportunity to work off their debts.

This management system teaches the students the responsibility of keeping track of their earnings and money paper. The reward of a piece of candy a week may seem to be a small one, but it is surprising how hard students will work toward that goal and for the recognition it gives.

Appendix C

*"How Am I Ever Going to Control this Class?"**

Other teachers quietly shake their heads, the principal has exhausted her supply of subtle hints and the teacher involved frequently goes home very close to tears, wondering, "How am I ever going to control these kids?" The lack of classroom discipline has driven more than one potentially promising but inexperienced teacher out of the education business.

The remedy? The Point Card. A simple, practical, and widely adaptable method for establishing effective behavior management without investing a lot of time, money, or energy. The Point Card is

POINT CARD	Coming in & Sitting Down Quietly	Beginning Work	Finishing Work	Not Bothering Your Neighbor	Being Polite
MONDAY					
TUESDAY					
WEDNESDAY					
THURSDAY					
FRIDAY					

based on five behaviors, which are depicted graphically at the top. To the side the days of the week are listed along with the student's name. Stickers, happy faces, checkmarks, etc., await at day's end for all achieved behaviors. Fridays bring extra free time, edibles, a movie, etc., to the completed card. Fewer points result in the reduction or elimination of the teacher-determined rewards.

I began this system several years ago when I was often very close to tears trying to teach mentally handicapped adolescents how to read. Since then the Point Card has been adopted in many special and regular classes serving Kindergarten through the eighth grade. Last year I was asked by my supervisor to present a workshop to describe many of the classroom materials I have developed. The Point Card generated much interest among participants and was later adopted by many of them.

*Reprinted with permission from K. Draper, "How am I ever going to control this class?" *The Directive Teacher,* Vol. 6, No. 2, Summer/Fall, 1984, p. 14.

Appendix D

Classroom Auctions: A Bonus for Students and Teacher*

"Going once. Going twice. Sold! One package of unicorn stickers for 1,050 points!"

"What is all that commotion?"

"Oh, that's just another auction down in Mrs. Fox's room. You know—the room with all those chocolate mobiles hanging from the ceiling."

Does this sound a little strange to you? It might. It is not the normal dialogue you would hear as you walk down the halls of an elementary school, but it is something you might hear as you pass by my room. I believe learning can be fun, and I strive to prove that to my students as often as possible.

I feel it is important for students to be actively involved in the learning process. There are several different approaches to being actively involved. It can mean using their names in sample sentences. I often do this when teaching the mechanics of writing sentences or in working on grammar lessons. They are much more interested when their names or their friend's names are used.

Active learning means everyone involved is active. I try to get them up and out of their chairs as often as possible. When teaching the concept of sets in math, we put students with certain characteristics (blue eyes, brown hair, those wearing tennis shoes, etc.) into "sets" in different parts of the room.

Being a somewhat dramatic person myself, I often encourage my students to put feeling into all that they do. They know that if they don't read with "pizzazz," I may pretend to fall asleep and start snoring. The things these poor children must endure!

*Reprinted from K. Fox, Classroom auction as a bonus for students and teacher, *Missouri Schools*, Missouri Department of Elementary and Secondary Education. February-March, 1985, p. 13.

A new method I began to use last year is the idea of an auction. I found that many students finished their morning seatwork rather quickly and then asked the ever-popular, oft-repeated question, "Now what can I do?" I had learning games and a fairly large selection of paperback books in the room. My problem was, I had moved up to fifth grade with my last year's fourth graders. They had read most of my books and played all of my games! Now what?

With a lot of encouragement and some out-and-out begging, I agreed to the ideas of an auction. One of the other fourth-grade teachers had used this method and was quite successful. I had toyed with the idea, but was somewhat reluctant to start something that would mean more work for me. But the students' enthusiasm convinced me, and I have never regretted one minute of it.

Approximately three days a week, I would put up "bonus point" work. It was always optional. The work included math activities, current events, language skills, riddles, crossword puzzles, etc. We also had monthly spelling worksheets. In addition, special units pertaining to student interests were assigned. Last year, units about the Olympics and chocolates were favorites. Parts of these units were required work, but I also included optional activities that would earn bonus points. All the points were recorded on a chart kept on the wall. Students tallied their points daily, even when they had not done any new work.

When the big day of the auction came, the students were so excited they could hardly control themselves. All students, as well as their teacher, donated items for the auction. They used bonus points they had earned to bid on precious items. Items for the auction ranged from used books and games to animal skulls and bones. There was even dinner and a hockey game with the teacher. (Some students were willing to bid more than 2,000 points for that.) The parents who came to observe were amazed to see some students bid more than 500 points on a package of Big League chewing gum. Everyone went home with something.

The first auction convinced more students to spend their "free time" doing extra work. They were practicing many needed skills, but without the complaining or the pressure of its being required. They didn't have to do it—they wanted to!

Appendix E

*Signs of Drug Use**

Changing patterns of performance, appearance, and behavior may signal use of drugs. The items in the first category listed below provide direct evidence of drug use; the items in the other categories offer signs that may indicate drug use. For this reason, adults should look for extreme changes in children's behavior, changes that together form a pattern associated with drug use.

Signs of Drugs and Drug Paraphernalia
1. Possession of drug-related paraphernalia such as pipes, rolling papers, small decongestant bottles, or small butane torches.
2. Possession of drugs or evidence of drugs, peculiar plants, or butts, seeds, or leaves in ashtrays or clothing pockets.
3. Odor of drugs, smell of incense or other "cover-up" scents.

Identification with Drug Culture
1. Drug-related magazines, slogans on clothing.
2. Conversation and jokes that are preoccupied with drugs.
3. Hostility in discussing drugs.

Signs of Physical Deterioration
1. Memory lapses, short attention span, difficulty in concentration.
2. Poor physical coordination, slurred or incoherent speech.
3. Unhealthy appearance, indifference to hygiene and grooming.
4. Bloodshot eyes, dilated pupils.

Dramatic Changes in School Performance
1. Distinct downward turns in student's grades—not just from Cs to Fs but from As to Bs and Cs. Assignments not completed.

2. Increased absenteeism or tardiness.

Changes in Behavior
1. Chronic dishonesty (lying, stealing, cheating). Trouble with the police.
2. Changes in friends, evasiveness in talking about new ones.
3. Possession of large amounts of money.
4. Increasing and inappropriate anger, hostility, irritability, secretiveness.
5. Reduced motivation, energy, self-discipline, self-esteem.
6. Diminished interest in extracurricular activities and hobbies.

*Reprinted from: *What Works: Schools Without Drugs*, U.S. Department of Education, 1986, p. 16.

Appendix F

Sample Contract

I, _____ , hereby declare that I will
    (student's name)

_____

(statement of what student has to do)

_____

_____ .

This job will be considered successfully completed when

_____

(statement of expected level of proficiency

_____

or quality of performance)

_____   _____

   Date signed   Student signature

By successfully completing the above activity, you may

_____ .

(statement of reward)

_____   _____

  Date completed   Teacher signature

Appendix G

Award Certificate

Certificate of Award

This Certifies That

is worthy of Special Recognition and Commendation for

and is therefore awarded this Certificate

This honor is conferred this   day of   19

Awarded at Will Beckley School

TEACHER   PRINCIPAL

Appendix H

Signal card*

Too frequently, students needing teacher assistance will raise and wave their hands, look up, and remain off task until they receive the teacher's attention. The following "describes a nondisruptive procedure for requesting assistance that also allows students to learn the efficient use of time and to develop independent work habits" (Paine et al, 1983, p. 110).

Fold the paper evenly into two 4-inch sections and two 2-inch sections. Print "Please Keep Working" on one 4-inch section. This side will face the student when the card is attached to the desk. On the other 4-inch section, print "Please Help Me." This side will face out toward the teacher. (You may write different messages if you prefer.) Then laminate the paper.

Next, fold the paper into a triangular shape with two 4-inch sides and a 2-inch base. Tape or staple the triangle together.

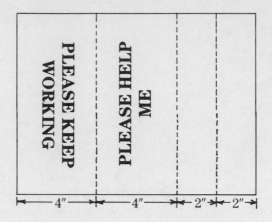

Attach the signs with 1½-inch strapping tape along the bottom edge of the "Please Help Me" (facing out) side and the outer edge of the students' desks. This allows the card to be raised or lowered easily.

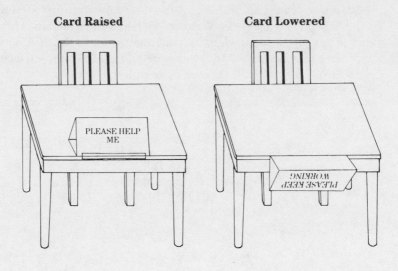

*reprinted with permission from Paine, S.C., Radicci, J., Rosellini, L.C., Deutchman, L., and Darch, C.B., *Structuring your classroom for academic success,* Champaign, Illinois: Research Press, 1983, pp. 111-112.

Appendix I

List of reinforcers

Verbal

Good
Neat
O.K.
Great
Charming
Commendable
Delightful
Brilliant
Fine answer
Uh-huh
Go ahead
All right
Correct
Excellent
Perfect
Satisfactory
Keep going
Good responses
Fantastic
Terrific
Marvelous
Nifty
Cool
Wonderful
Outstanding Work
Fabulous
That's clever
I'm pleased

Thank you
That shows thought
We think a lot of you
You're tops on our list
That's good work
Remarkably well done
That shows a great deal of work
Yes, I think you should continue
That is a feather in your cap
That's a nice expression
That's an excellent goal
That's interesting
You make being a teacher very
    worthwhile
Well thought out
Show us how
You're going better
I'm so proud of you
I like that thinking

Body Expressions

Patting shoulder
Hugging
Shaking hands
Squeezing hand
Walking alongside
Gently raising chin
Putting face next to child
Tweaking nose

Eating with children
Interacting with class at recess
Smiling
Winking
Nodding
Grinning
Signaling o.k.
Giving thumbs up
Shaking head
Shrugging shoulders
Widening eyes
Wrinkling nose

Tangible

Tokens
Praise
Free time
Extra recess
Self-graphing
Daily good reports to parents
Food
Candy
Extra art time
Field trips
Messenger boy or girl
Party after school
Class proctor
Soda
Nurse's helper
Cafeteria helper
Library time
Extra reading (free reading)
Stars on a paper
Papers on wall
Get to sit by friend
Class leader to bathroom
Class leader to cafeteria
Pat on back by teacher
Happy faces on papers

Name on board
Chance to help other students
No homework
Music teacher helper
Longer lunch periods
Choose a game
Points towards prize
Game equipment manager
Clean chalk board
Stamps on a hand
Stars on a chart
Read to younger children
Listen to records
Flag raiser
Honor roll
Grades
First for show and tell
Sharpen pencils for class
Ribbons
Puzzles
Comics
Jacks
Yo-yos
Small plastic toy
Jumping beans
Wax lips
Address books
Silly putty
Stuffed animal
Record
Pencil sharpener
Coloring book
Surprise package
Pins
Patches
First in line
Group leader
"Today's Best Kid"
"Citizen of the Week"
Competing with other classes

Early dismissal

Written

Bravo
Fine
Good
Neat
Very good
O.K.
Thoughtful
100 percent
Good paper
Very colorful
Well done
Great
Wow
A-1
Perceptive
Right-on
Correct
+
Satisfactory
Nicely done
Very concise
Complete
A, B, C, D
Excellent
Outstanding
Superior
Congratulations

Appendix J

Behavior Blossom (source unknown)

During homeroom on Monday morning, elementary students are provided copies of the attached "blossom." They are instructed to do the following:

— Color it
— Print name
— Date it
— Partially cut each petal so that, if necessary, a petal can be easily removed.

After the classroom rules are reviewed, students are told that their week's citizenship grades will be determined by the petals remaining on the blossoms. They are instructed that each time a student breaks a rule, he or she will be given a signal to remove a petal: first the A+ petal, then the A petal, then the B+ petal, and so forth. The best petal (highest grade) remaining on the blossom at the week's end will be each student's citizenship grade. A chart can be posted showing the weekly citizenship grades of all students during the semester.

Should this technique follow the use of "Conduct Countdown" (see Appendix K), it will be necessary to remind the class that they do not have as many chances to keep a high citizenship grade.

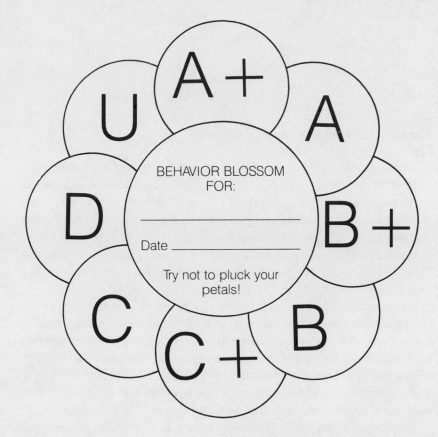

BEHAVIOR BLOSSOM
FOR:

_____

Date _____

Try not to pluck your
petals!

Appendix K

Conduct Countdown (source unknown)

Conduct countdown is a way of reducing the number of undesirable behaviors that often occur in the classroom. Before beginning this program, the teacher should inform students of the rules they will be expected to follow while the countdown is in effect. When the teacher says, "Conduct countdown is in effect," all students are to behave. During this special period of time, students should be closely observed to see that all their behaviors are appropriate. Not following through properly will ruin the effect of this device.

The student who does not follow the rules will have to suffer the consequences and must cut one strip from a slip on which grades are indicated in strips: see illustration. Each letter grade is divided by a line, and the cut will be made along one of the lines. The motion of moving two fingers as if cutting something can be used to inform a student of a rule violation and the need to cut off a strip. The teacher may also simply tell the student to cut off one strip.

Students with a letter grade of a B or less at the end of the week must take their conduct slip home and have their parents sign it and return it. This slip is given to the students at the beginning of the week. The resulting citizenship grade at the end of the week depends on the student's behavior.

Letters should be sent to each parent at the beginning of this management program to inform the parent of the actions being taken by the teacher to help with problems. This letter will help parents become included in the program. It will probably also help them grade the program successfully.

At the top of the slip is a place for the student's name, the date, the parent's signature, and the teacher or parent's comments. Students should keep the slips taped to their desks.

CONDUCT COUNTDOWN GRADE

FOR:

_____

Name

_____

Date

Parent's Signature: _____

Comments: _____

U
D –
D
D +
C –
C
C +
B –
B
B +
A –
A
A +

Appendix L

Learnball

Learnball is an instructional management system guaranteed to increase motivation, productivity, and self-discipline—and to decrease discipline problems. The Learnball approach uses peer social approval as a reward. A foam ball and a hoop are used to create an appealing sports format, and classroom rules become the rules of the sport (Marwood, McMullen, and Murray, 1986, p. 57). Learnball involves cooperative teamwork with students winning points of varying amounts based on the accuracy and achievement levels of their work and answers. The one point earned by a slower student may win the contest.

In implementing the system, the class votes to form two balanced learning teams, after which the teams and teacher work within a system characterized by the following:

1. An agreement to adhere to rules
2. An election of fellow students to positions of team leaders, assistant teacher, score keeper, and quarter master
3. An establishment of point values for rules agreed to by students and teachers
4. Teams earning points for being prepared, following directions, completing work, answering questions, participating in learning activities, and following rules
5. The use of a foam ball as a reward for work
6. The issuance of merit awards

There is a network of Learnball enthusiasts making up the Learnball League International. This group supports its members through a newsletter and a telephone hotline. The league promises to refund the membership fee if the system fails to decrease discipline problems or to improve motivation. Teachers wishing more information should read the following references or send a business-size, self-addressed, stamped envelope to Learnball League, P.O. Box 18221, Pleasant Hills, PA 15236. See also Bradley (1970), Marwood, McMullen, and Murray (1986), and Sneed (1983).

Appendix M

Other Managerial Techniques

Discouraging slowness of work

Draw up a contingency contract to discourage slowness in work. The contract should specify that students are not required to complete the last third of the assignment if they finish the first two-thirds within a certain amount of time. The contract should also contain a proficiency criterion to discourage incorrect work. Naturally, there must be other worthy learning activities for the early finishers. A variation of this technique is to merely terminate the seatwork after a reasonable time with those having finished being excused from homework. Those who did not finish are to complete their assignment as homework.

Discouraging forgotten assignments

Teachers sometimes use the "Let's Make a Deal" approach in discouraging incomplete assignments and forgotten work supplies. The teacher, after picking five students' names from a box, asks each to produce two items previously listed on the board (completed assignment, pencil, specific resource book, Newsweek, etc.). Students producing the items are immediately reinforced with a token, candy, etc. The procedure could be modified by also imposing a fine on those not prepared for the upcoming lesson.

Decreasing transition time

It is a good procedure for teachers to periodically keep track of the time spent on transitions. Should the tally reveal that excessive time is being spent by students in transition, then make a contract with the class: time saved in transitions during the week will be saved and used for a special activity on Friday.

Discouraging out-of-seat behavior

Record a soft tone at three- to five-minute intervals on an audio tape. Play the recording during seatwork while listening for the periodic tone. Record an "O.K." if everyone is seated and record a "NO" if someone is not seated. Gather your data over a few days in an attempt to learn the seriousness of the problem. If a significant problem exists, develop a contract with the class which states what they will receive according to the number of "O.K.s" and "NOs" the class receives: that is, so many seconds or minutes for each recorded "O.K." provides something and each "NO" takes something away. Make a second tape with intervals of varying lengths to discourage students from "learning" when to be seated.

Token system using profile face

Make a "profile face" or a large name card, with an attached pocket, for each student. Attach these to a wall or bulletin board. After identifying a behavior that you want improved, inform the students that a token will be placed into the "pockets" of all students doing the desired behavior. The tokens, which will be given at previously determined intervals, can later be traded for desirable items and privileges. This technique could also be used with only one student.

Reward for less noise

Inform the students that for every five minutes that the class (or a single student) is quiet and on task, a plus (+) will be placed in a circle on the chalkboard. Likewise, a minus sign (-) will be added should the noise level (or talking of an individual student) become too great or too frequent. Each plus earns two minutes of special activity on Friday. Some teachers impose a fine for the minus signs: a reduction in time for some desired activity.

Signaling for quiet time

If students are seated in rows, require them to pivot their chairs for different activities. For instance, students face one wall during seatwork when they are allowed to ask "constructive" questions and give constructive answers to each other. When it is time for them to not converse and to listen to your presentation, they pivot their chairs 90 degrees to face you and the chalkboard.

Beads as positive reinforcers

First, purchase an assortment of inexpensive beads and string. Issue one bead to each student who shows the desired behavior. The beads are temporarily placed into a small enclosed container until the end of the day, when they are added to the necklace. The necklace may be traded in for another reinforcer, or it may be kept.

Comments on secondary students' papers

Although almost everyone appreciates kind and congratulatory words, some recipients of "traditional" compliments ("Nice work, James") receive teasing comments from their peers. One secondary teacher found it better to give more "mod" compliments: "Right on," "Groovy," "I dig your approach," etc.

Improving dismissals

Some teachers find themselves giving threats, shouting, and having to assist students as they prepare for dismissal. One teacher decided to change her behavior in an attempt to get students to change. She made herself a pledge to announce *one* time that the dismissal bell will ring in two minutes and what the state of readiness must be before students will be allowed to exit. She then busied herself, became stoic, and ignored the excessive noise and lack of preparation for dismissal. The class was finally released four minutes after the bell. By consistently following this procedure in the ensuing days, peer pressure helped the teacher bring about readiness on the students' part. They became more self-disciplined, more self-reliant.

Jug rewarding system

You may wish to show students your appreciation for good behavior. After reviewing the few classroom rules and expressing a desire to reward the class for good behavior, call the students' attention to an aquarium or gallon jug and an accompanying container of marbles. Explain that periodically, when the class is on task and obeying the rules, you will drop a marble into the container. At the end of the day, the marbles will be counted and multiplied by thirty seconds. The accumulated time may be used for highly stimulating activities such as fifteen minutes of "Simon

Says," a twenty-minute popcorn party, twenty-five minutes for a spelling contest, etc.

A roll of inexpensive tickets can be used to issue tokens of appreciation for good behavior. The tickets can be accumulated by students, and, when a certain number has been saved, those with that number may reach in a "grab bag" and pull out a card specifying an award. Naturally, the drawing and issuing of rewards will occur only at predetermined times. Possible rewards may include two extra points on the next quiz, a ticket to the high school game or play, free time, a candy bar, listening to "rock tape," etc. (Canter, 1979, p. 2).

Handling visitors

Anticipate periodic interruptions and have an approach for minimizing the loss of instructional time. Inform your students during the first week what to do when visitors (parents, janitor, nurse, secretary, principal, etc.) come to the classroom. Additionally, you should:

> Greet visitor and invite him or her into the room.
> Position yourself so that you can keep eye contact with the class while speaking to the visitor.
> If the interruption is expected to last more than a few seconds, excuse yourself to the visitor and inform the students of their work assignment (continue their assignment, free reading, next two problems, start of tomorrow's homework, etc.).

Should the visitor want more than a few minutes of your time, courteously advise him or her of your need to continue supervising and instructing the class and schedule a conference during your planning or conference period. Should the visitor be unauthorized or emotionally upset, it may be necessary to send for assistance or to ask the teacher in the adjoining room to "supervise" your students while you escort the visitor away from the children and toward the office.

Eliminating pencil sharpening

Pencil sharpening may cost valuable instructional time unless there is an adhered-to system. Some teachers issue two or three pencils that are to be sharpened before class or at another designated time. Other teachers begin each day with a receptacle of sharpened pencils from which each student receives one pencil. A student may receive a second pencil should his or her lead become dull or break, but the pencil sharpener is not operated during the instructional segments of the school day.

Bulletin board for reinforcing behavior

A "Shoot for the Moon" bulletin board can be used for reinforcing good behavior. The board is covered with blue paper (sky), cutouts of clouds, and a prominent smiling moon. Small 1/2-inch spaceship cutouts, each with a student's name, are aligned at the bottom and are advanced 1/2 inch towards the moon each time the teacher observes a previously specified desired behavior. A teacher may wish to include a negative consequence (moving downward) for misbehaviors such as being noisy in the lunchroom, having an incomplete assignment, etc. A deadline for reaching the moon is announced; those arriving on the moon by a certain date become participants in some special activity (popcorn party, etc.) or recipients of some item (picture of astronauts obtained from NASA, etc.). Faint lines may be drawn across the blue background paper to facilitate the accurate movement of the spaceships (Evertson et al., 1981, p. 62).

Hourglass for dismissing students

An hourglass may be used for dismissing students following an explanation that it takes three minutes for the sand to run through and that the "glass" will be turned over each day at three minutes before the dismissal bell. The class is further informed that if they are all prepared for dismissal before the sand runs through, they may quietly exit ahead of the other rooms—with the first prepared being the first in line. Should the class not be ready by the bell, the class will remain in session until all "chores" (previously explained) are complete (Evertson et al., 1981, p. 85).

Student monitors

Teachers sometimes use their students as assistants to help with routines in the classroom. These assistants or monitors are asked to assume their positions and to consistently fulfill the assigned responsibilities. Monitors receive recognition by their assignments and by the posting of their names and positions, and they also learn to accept responsibility. Although student monitors can be of help in servicing managerial routines, teachers must realize that they will have to spend time selecting, training, and in monitoring the monitors (Charles, 1983, p. 71-72). Below are some examples of monitors:

Messenger: responsible to deliver messages.

PE monitor: responsible for distributing, collecting, and storing recess equipment.

Flag monitor: responsible for coordinating the flag salute.

Line monitor: responsible for acting as a good model in lining up to exit or enter classrooms, lunchroom, buses, etc. This person usually heads up his or her line and exemplifies punctuality and good manners.

Group monitors: responsible for distributing and collecting materials and encouraging the group to be responsible for their work area.

Biologist: responsible for caring for classroom plants and animals.

Visitor monitors: responsible for greeting visitors, introducing them to the teacher, and escorting them to the office or exit after their visit.

A-V monitor: responsible for helping obtain, operate, and return audio-visual equipment.

Substitute teacher monitor: responsible for always knowing assignments, lesson topics, location of teacher's handbook and lesson plans, and for helpfully communicating this information to substitute teachers.

Signal systems

Two techniques for assisting seatworkers are offered by Nancy Buckley and Hill Walker:

One system is for each child to have a small tag (attached to his desk or inside his desk) that can be placed on top of the desk to signal the need for help. Thus, the child has his hands free to continue working, by prior agreement, the teacher will go first to those children who are working.

A second system involves a series of numbers at the teacher's desk such as are found in many department store catalogue departments. The first child waiting for help takes Number 1, the second child Number 2, and so on; then they return to their seat to work. As the teacher finishes helping one child she calls out the next number (1978, p. 30).

The second system, though novel, has two handicapping features: it requires more student movement and it requires the teacher to call out the next number. Both of these features are disruptive influences. (A third "signaling" approach is illustrated in Appendix H.)

Clothespins to check roll

Some teachers start each day by checking roll and then directly moving into the lesson, while others employ varying techniques. Charles (1983, p. 68) describes a procedure whereby clothespins containing students' names are clipped onto a board by the classroom door. Upon entering the room, each student removes his or her pin and attaches it to another chart containing his or her name and designating his or her immediate task assignment. This procedure also tells the teacher who is absent by the clothespins remaining by the door.

An activity commonly used for starting the day is uninterrupted sustained silent reading (USSR). Each student, upon entering the room, knows to remain silent and to continue reading his or her library book. *Both* the students and the teacher continue to read for approximately twenty minutes.

Passport for reinforcement

A passport system may be used to reinforce a child's good behavior and to maintain communications among parents, teachers, and other adults responsible for supervising a child's behavior. All involved parties, including the child, are informed of the system— which has the following particulars (adapted from Runge, Walker, and Shea, 1975):

1. The child is rewarded for carrying a special notebook and presenting it to appropriate adults. The involved adults will minimally include the teacher and parents and possibly other adults, such as the bus driver, music teacher, and supervisors outside the building.
2. All involved adults are to make notations in the passport—a spiral notebook.

3. Points (tokens) are awarded to the child for specified behaviors according to a predetermined reinforcement schedule. A "menu" provides the relative value cost of various rewards. The rewards may be furnished by the parents or guardians.
4. A point card is affixed to the inside of the notebook's front cover.
5. In making notations, all involved adults are to
   a. be brief
   b. be consistent by making an entry each day
   c. be honest, but not overly negative: that is, rather than write a scathing note, ask for a parent conference to discuss behavior

Daily report cards

It appears that our system of issuing report cards every six or nine weeks has a positive effect on students' performance—but only immediately before and after the cards are issued (Walker and Shea, 1984, p. 91). If report cards have only a short-term effect, why not issue daily report cards for modifying social behavior and academic performance?

A system developed by Dickerson et al. (1973, pp. 170-178), called the "Teacher-Parent Communication Program" (TPCP), instructs the teacher to issue report cards approximately every forty minutes throughout the school day.

Daily Report Card

_____ School work satisfactory   _____ Social behavior satisfactory

_____ School work unsatisfactory _____ Social behavior unsatisfactory

Teacher: _____ Date: _____

Notation: _____

The major points of TPCP should be explained to the parents and the student so that all involved persons understand both their duties and their responsibilities. Parents, on the basis of the cards' information, will reward or not reward the child for the day's school performance. A reward is never issued unless the teacher checks both the social and academic performance as being acceptable. The number of acceptable cards required for a reward and the performance level required before a teacher will mark the card acceptable is mutually agreed to by the parent and the teacher and explained to the child. "As the child's overall level of performance increases, the number of acceptable cards needed for rewards is systematically increased" (Walker and Shea, 1984, p. 195). Parents have a wealth of rewards, privileges, and tasks in the home that can be granted, denied, or assigned.

1. Determine the number of cards to be sent home each day.
2. One "unsatisfactory" mark makes a card unacceptable.
3. Each card is signed by the teacher and is free of changes or erasures.
4. The program will initially emphasize the quantity of work, and later the quality of work.
5. Weekend bonuses may be given for a previously agreed-upon number of perfect cards.
6. The child's after-school activities should be daily affected by his or her performance in school (cards).
7. A parent or guardian will analyze the cards immediately after school and determine the child's rewards, restrictions, or tasks. Cards not received by parents are counted as unacceptable.
8. After the system is once initiated, the resulting consequences are determined by the child's behavior. Therefore, "let the cards talk." Praise the child for good performance but do not lecture him or her on unsatisfactory performances.
9. Parents and teachers should meet and confer at least weekly.

Different rules for different activities

Marlene and Lee Canter (1976, pp. 65-66) warn teachers that "no matter what the activity, in order to be assertive, you need to be aware of what behaviors you want and need from the students." With this in mind, teachers employing a variety of activities may find it helpful to categorize the different instructional and activity time segments and post the three or four most important behaviors or needs. Elementary teachers may find it desirable to use five or six different signs during a day.

Transitions
1. Follow directions
2. No talking
3. Quickly get on new task or lesson

Lecture
1. No talking without permission
2. Take notes
3. Maintain same pacing as teacher

Quiet work
1. Follow posted explanations
2. No talking or being out of chair
3. Completed work will be picked up
4. Early finishers begin on homework or free read

Group work
1. Remain in assigned group
2. Low, constructive talk allowed
3. One designated person from each group is responsible for obtaining the group's supplies. This student is allowed to be on the floor when no other class member is up.
4. Each person is responsible for the work and must turn in the assigned work unless otherwise instructed.

References

Chapter 1

Baker, K. (1985). Research evidence of a school discipline problem. *Phi Delta Kappan*, March, 482-488.

Bartlett, L. (1985). Legal responsiblities of students: Study shows school officials also win court decisions. *NAASP Bulletin*, March, pp. 39-47.

Bauer, G.L. (1985). Restoring order to the public schools. *Phi Delta Kappan*, March, pp. 488-490.

Benard, B., B. Fagoglia, and J. Perone (1987). Know what to do—and not to do—reinvigorates drug education. *ASCD Curriculum Update*, February, pp. 1-12.

Gallup, A.M. (1986). The 18th annual Gallup poll of the public's attitudes toward the public schools. *Phi Delta Kappan*, September, pp. 43-59.

Gallup, G.H. (1984). The 16th annual Gallup poll of the public's attitudes toward the public schools. *Phi Delta Kappan*, September, pp. 23-38.

Harris, L., and Associates (1984). *Metropolitan life survey of the American teacher.* New York: Lou Harris and Associates.

Jones, F.H. (1979). The gentle art of classroom discipline. *National Elementary Principal*, June, pp. 26-32.

National Education Association (1983). *Teacher opinion poll.* Washington, D.C.: National Education Association.

National Institute of Education (1978). *In violent schools: The safe school study report to Congress*, Vol. 1, Washington, D.C.: U.S. Dept. of Health, Education, and Welfare.

National Institute of Education (1983). *Violent schools, safe schools: The safe school study report to the Congress.* Washington, D.C.: National Institute of Education.

National School Safety Center (1985). *School safety and the legal community.* Sacramento, California: National School Safety Center.

Noble, E.P. (ed.) (1978). *Third special report to the U.S. Congress on alcohol and health.* Rockville, Maryland: National Institute of Alcohol Abuse and Alcoholism.

Ryan, K. (1986). The new moral education. *Phi Delta Kappan,* November, pp. 228-233.

Sawyer, K.A. (1983). *The right to safe schools: A newly recognized inalienable right.* Sacramento, California: National School Safety Center.

U.S. Department of Education (1986). *What works: Schools without drugs.* Washington, D.C.: U.S. Department of Education.

Wayson, W.W. (1985). The politics of violence in school: Doublespeak and disruptions in public confidence. Phi Delta Kappan, October, pp. 127-132.

Weiner, J. (1985). Peer power. *Family Weekly,* April, p. 4.

Chapter 2

Arbuthnot, J.B., and D. Faust (1981). *Teaching moral reasoning: Theory and practice.* New York: Harper and Row.

Becker, W.C. (1971). *Parents are teachers: A child management program.* Champaign, Illinois: Research Press.

Becker, W.C., S. Engelmann, and D.R. Thomas (1971). *Teaching: A course in applied psychology.* Chicago: Science Research Associates.

Berne, E. (1972). *What do you say after you say hello? The Psychology of human destiny.* New York: Grove Press.

Boules, A. (ed.) (1981). *Crossroads: A handbook for effective classroom management.* New York: Harper and Row.

Buckley, N.K., and H.M. Walker (1978). *Modifying classroom behavior: A manual of procedure for classroom teachers.* Champaign, Illinois: Research Press.

Canter, L., and M. Canter (1976). *Assertive discipline: A take charge approach for today's educator.* Los Angeles: Canter and Associates.

Canter, L. (1979). *Assertive discipline: Competency based guidelines and resource materials.* Los Angeles: Canter and Associates.

_____ (1984). *Assertive discipline: Secondary resource material workbook (grades 7-12).* Santa Monica, California: Canter and Associates, Inc.

_____ (1986). *Assertive discipline: Phase 2 Teacher Workbook.* Santa Monica, California: Canter and Associates, Inc.

Charles, C.M. (1981). *Building classroom discipline: From models to practice.* New York: Longman.

Charles, C.M. (1983). *Elementary classroom management.* New York: Longman.

Charles, C.M. (1985). *Building classroom discipline: From models to practice.* New York: Longman.

Curwin, R.L., and A.N. Mendler (1980). *The discipline book: A complete guide to school and classroom management.* Reston, Virginia: Reston Publishing.

Dreikurs, R., B.B. Grunwald, and F.C. Pepper (1982). *Maintaining sanity in the classroom.* New York: Harper and Row.

Duke, D.L. (1986). Understanding what it means to be a teacher. *Educational Leadership,* Vol. 44, No. 2, October, pp. 26-32.

Fernald, L.D., and P.S. Fernald (1978). *Introduction to psychology.* Geneva, Illinois: Houghton Mifflin.

Gardner, H. (1982). *Development psychology: An introduction.* Boston: Little, Brown.

Gerow, J.R. (1986). *Psychology: An introduction.* Glenview, Illinois: Scott, Foresman.

Ginott, H. (1972). *Teacher and child.* New York: Macmillan.

Glasser, W. (1969). *Schools without failure.* New York: Harper and Row.

_____ (1978). *Glasser's 10 steps to discipline.* Hollywood, California: Media Five.

_____ (1986). Recent advances in reality therapy. Presentation at a conference of the Child Advocacy Council of Joplin, Missouri, April.

Gnagey, W.J. (1981). *Motivating classroom discipline.* New York: Macmillan.

Gordon, T. (1974). *T.E.T.: Teacher effectiveness training.* New York: David McKay, Inc.

_____ (1984). *T.E.T.: Teacher effectiveness training.* New York: David McKay.

References

Howell, R.G., Jr., and P.L. Howell (1979). *Discipline in the classroom: Solving the teaching puzzle.* Reston, Virginia: Reston Publishing.

James, M., and D. Jongeward (1976). *Born to win: Transactional analysis with gestalt experiments.* Barrington, Illinois: Addison-Wesley.

Jones, F.H. (1979). The gentle art of classroom discipline. *National Elementary Principal,* June, pp. 26-32.

Kohlberg, L., and R.H. Hersh (1985). Moral development: A review of the theory. In J.M. Rich (ed.), *Innovations in education: Reformers and their critics* (pp. 225-235). Boston: Allyn and Bacon.

Maslow, A.H. (1970). *Motivation and personality* (2nd ed.). New York: Harper and Row.

Nucci, L. (1987). Synthesis of research on moral development. *Educational Leadership,* Vol. 44, No. 5, February, pp. 86-92.

O'Leary, S.G., and K.D. O'Leary (1976). Behavior modification in the school. In H. Leitenberg (ed.), *Handbook of behavior modification and behavior* (pp. 475-485). Englewood Cliffs, New Jersey: Prentice-Hall.

Raths, L., et al. (1978). *Values and teaching* (2nd ed.). Columbus, Ohio: Charles E. Merrill.

Rich, J.M. (ed.) (1985). *Innovations in education: Reformers and their critics.* Boston: Allyn and Bacon.

Rogers, C. (1951). *Client-centered therapy.* Boston: Houghton Mifflin.

———— (1968). Significant learning: In therapy and in education. In Hyman, R.T. (ed.), *Teaching: Vantage Points for Study* (pp. 152-165). New York: J.B. Lippincott.

Ryan, K. (1986). The new moral education. *Phi Delta Kappan,* Vol. 68, No. 4, November, pp. 228-233.

Skinner, B.F. (1986). Programmed instruction revisited. *Phi Delta Kappan,* October, pp. 103-110.

Sloane, H.N. (1976). *Classroom management: Remediation and prevention.* New York: John Wiley.

Walker, J.E., and T.M. Shea (1984). *Behavior management: A practical approach for educators.* St. Louis, Missouri: Times Mirror/Mosby College Publishing.

Wallen, C.J., and L.L. Wallen (1978). *Effective classroom management.* Boston: Allyn and Bacon.

Wolfgang, C.H., and C.D. Glickman (1980). *Solving discipline problems.* Boston: Allyn and Bacon.

Wong, H.K. (1986). How to achieve maximum success in the classroom. Southwest District meeting of the Missouri State Teacher's Association. Springfield, Missouri, October.

Chapter 3

Introduction

Barth, Roland S. (1985). Outside looking in—Inside looking in. *Phi Delta Kappan*, January, pp. 356-358.

Berliner, D.C. (1984). The half-full class: A review of research on teaching. In P.L. Hosford (ed.), *Using what we know about teaching* (pp. 51-77). Alexandria, Virginia: Association for Supervision and Curriculum Development.

Good, T.L., and D. Grouws (1979). The Missouri mathematics effectiveness project: An experimental study in fourth-grade classrooms. *Journal of Educational Psychology*, Vol. 71, pp. 355-362.

National Commission on Excellence in Education (1983). *A Nation at risk: The imperative for educational reform.* Superintendent of Documents, U.S. Printing Office, Washington, D.C. 20402, April.

Paine, S.C., et al. (1983). *Structuring your classroom for academic success.* Champaign, Illinois: Research Press.

Rosenholtz, S.J. (1985). Political myths about education reform: Lessons from research on teaching. *Phi Delta Kappan*, January, pp. 349-354.

Schlechty, P.C. (1985). Evaluation procedures in the Charlotte-Mecklenburg career ladder plan. *Educational Leadership*, pp. 14-19.

U.S. Department of Education (1986). *What works: Research about teaching and learning.* Pueblo, Colorado.

Expectations, attitudes, and emphasis

Brookover, W., et al. (1978). Elementary school social climate and school achievement. *American Educational Research Journal, Vol. 15*, pp. 301-318.

Brophy, J., and C. Evertson (1976). *Learning from teaching: A developmental perspective.* Boston: Allyn and Bacon.

References

Fisher, C.W., et al. (1981). Teaching behavior, academic learning time and student achievement: An overview. *Journal of Classroom Interaction, Vol. 17, No. 1,* pp. 2-15.

Good, T., and J. Brophy (1978). *Looking in classrooms* (2nd ed.). New York: Harper and Row.

Medley, D.M. (1979). The effectiveness of teachers. In Peterson and Walberg (eds.), *Research on Teaching.* Berkeley, California: McCutchan.

Ornstein, A.C. (1981). Teacher behavior research: Overview and outlook. *Phi Delta Kappan,* April, pp. 592-596.

Rutter, M., et al. (1979). *Fifteen thousand hours.* Cambridge, Massachusetts: Harvard University Press.

Schwille, J., et al. (1981). *Teachers as policy brokers in the content of elementary school mathematics.* National Institute of Education (Contract No. P-80-0127). East Lansing: Institute for Research on Teaching, Michigan State University.

Soar, R.S., D.M. Medley, and H. Coker (1983). Teacher evaluation: A critique of currently used methods. *Phi Delta Kappan,* December, pp. 239-246.

Soar, R.S., and R.M. Soar (1973). *Classroom behavior, pupil characteristics and pupil growth for the school year and the summer.* Florida: Institute for Development of Human Resources. College of Education, University of Florida, Gainesville, Florida.

Consequences

Broden, M., et al. (1970). Effects of teacher attention on attending behavior of two boys at adjacent desks. *Journal of Applied Behavior Analysis, Vol. 3,* pp. 199-203.

Fisher, C.W., et al. (1980). Teaching behavior, academic learning time, and student achievement: An overview. *Time to learn.* Washington, D.C.: National Institute of Education, May, pp. 7-32.

Forehand, R., et al. (1976). An examination of disciplinary procedures with children. *Journal of Experimental Child Psychology, Vol. 21,* pp. 109-120.

Gordon, I.J., and R.E. Jester (1973). Techniques of observing teaching in early childhood and outcomes of particular procedures. In Robert M. Travers (ed.), *Secondary Handbook of Research on Teaching.* Chicago: Rand McNally.

Kash, M.M., and E.D. Borich (1978). *Teacher behavior and pupil self-concept.* Reading, Massachusetts: Addison-Wesley.

Kazdin, A.E. (1973). The effect of vicarious reinforcement on attentive behavior in the classroom. *Journal of Applied Behavior Analysis, Vol. 6,* pp. 71-78.

Kounin, J., and P. Gump (1961). The comparative influence of punitive and nonpunitive teachers upon children's concepts of school misconduct. *Journal of Educational Psychology, Vol. 52,* pp. 44-49.

Lasley, T. (1981). Research perspectives on classroom management. *Journal of Teacher Education, Vol. 32, No. 2,* pp. 14-17.

O'Leary, K., et al. (1969). A token reinforcement program in a public school: A replication and systematic analysis. *Journal of Applied Behavior Analysis, Vol. 1,* pp. 3-13.

Rohrkemper, M., and J. Brophy (1980). Teachers' general strategies for dealing with problem students. Paper presented at the American Educational Research Association meeting, Boston, March.

Solomon, D., and A.J. Kendall (1976). *Final report: Individual characteristics and children's performance in varied educational settings.* Chicago: Spencer Foundation Project, May.

Walker, H., H. Hops, and E. Fiegenbaum (1976). Deviant classroom behavior as a function of combinations of social and token reinforcement and cost contingency. *Behavior Therapy, Vol. 7,* pp. 76-88.

Instructional methods

American Association of School Administrations (1982). *Time on task; Using instructional time more effectively.* Arlington, Virginia: American Association of School Administrations.

Anderson, L.M., C.M. Evertson, and J.E. Brophy (1979). An experimental study of effective teaching in first-grade reading groups. *Elementary School Journal, Vol. 79,* pp. 193-222.

Brophy, J., and C. Evertson (1976). *Learning from teaching: A developmental perspective.* Newton, Maryland: Allyn and Bacon.

Brophy, J.E., and J.C. Putnam (1978). Classroom management in the elementary grades. In D. Duke (ed.), *Classroom management* (pp. 182-216). Chicago: University of Chicago Press.

Fisher, C.W., et al. (1980). Teaching behaviors, academic learning time and student achievement: An overview. In C. Denham and A. Lieberman (eds.), *Time to learn* (pp. 7-32). Washington, D.C.: U.S. Department of Education, National Institute of Education.

Good, T.L. (1982). Classroom research: What we know or what we need to know. *Research in teacher education.* Report No. 9018. Research and Development Center for Teacher Education, The University of Texas, February.

McFaul, S.A. (1983). An examination of direct instruction. *Educational Leadership*, April, pp. 67-69.

Stallings, J. (1980). Allocated academic learning time revisited, or beyond time on task. *Educational Researcher,* December.

Monitoring

Doyle, W. (1980). *Classroom management.* West Lafayette, Indiana: Kappa Delta Pi, pp. 1-31.

Evertson, C.M., E.T. Emmer, and J.E. Brophy (1980). Predictors of effective teaching in junior high mathematics classrooms. *Journal of Research in Mathematics Education, Vol. II*, pp. 167-178.

Gump, P.V. (1969). Intra-setting analysis: The third-grade classroom as a special but instructive case. In E. Williams and H. Raush (eds.), *Naturalistic Viewpoints in Psychological Research* (pp. 200-220). New York: Holt, Rinehart and Winston.

Seatwork

Anderson, L.M., C.M. Evertson, and J.E. Brophy (1979). An experimental study of effective teaching in first-grade reading groups. *Elementary School Journal, Vol. 79*, pp. 193-222.

Angus, M.J., K.W. Evans, and B. Parkin (1975). *An observational study of selected pupil and teacher behavior in open plan and conventional design classrooms.* Australian open area project, Technical Report No. 4. Perth, Australia: Educational Department of Western Australia.

Eaton, J. (1984). Research on teaching. *Educational Leadership*, March, pp. 95-96.

Evertson, C., et al. (1980). Relationship between classroom behaviors and student outcomes in junior high mathematics and English classes. *American Educational Research Journal, Vol. 17*, pp. 43-60.

Fisher, C.W., et al. (1980). Teaching behaviors, academic learning time and student achievement: An overview. In C. Denham and A. Lieberman (eds.), *Time to learn* (pp. 7-32). Washington, D.C.: U.S. Department of Education, National Institute of Education.

Fisher, C.W., et al. (1978). *Teaching behaviors, academic learning time and student achievement.* Final Report of Phase III-B, Beginning Teacher Evaluation Study, Technical Report V-1. San Francisco, California: Far West Laboratory for Educational Research and Development.

Good, T.L., and D. Grouws (1978). The Missouri mathematics effectiveness project: An experimental study in fourth-grade classrooms. *Journal of Educational Psychology, Vol. 71*, pp. 355-362.

McDonald, F.J. (1976). *Research on teaching and its implications for policy making: Report on phase II of the beginning evaluation study.* Princeton, N.J.: Educational Testing Service.

Time allocations

Ayllon, T., S. Garber, and K. Pisor (1976). Reducing time limits: A means to increase behavior of retardates. *Journal of Applied Behavior Analysis, Vol. 9*, pp. 247-252.

Fisher, C.W., et al. (1981). Teaching behavior, academic learning time, and student achievement: An overview. *Journal of Classroom Interaction, Vol. 17, No. 1*, Winter, pp. 2-15.

Ornstein, A.C., and D.V. Levine (1983). Teacher behavior research: Overview and outlook. *Phi Delta Kappan*, April, p. 594.

Soar, R. (1978). *Setting variables, classroom interaction, multiple pupil outcomes.* Paper presented at the Annual Meeting of the American Educational Research Association, Toronto, Canada, April.

Stallings, J. (1975). Implementation and child effects of teaching practices in Follow Through classrooms. *Monographs of the Society for Research in Child Development, Vol. 40* (Serial No. 163).

Stallings, J., M. Needels, and N. Stayrook (1979). *The teaching of basic reading skills in secondary schools, phase II and phase III.* Menlo Park, California: SRI International.

Managerial

Emmer, E., C. Evertson, and L. Anderson (1979). *Effective classroom management at the beginning of the school year.* Research and Development Center for Teacher Education, University of Texas.

Good, T.L. (1982). Classroom research: What we know or what we need to know. *Research in teacher education.* Report No. 9018. Research and Development Center for Teacher Education, The University of Texas, February.

Kounin, J. (1977). *Discipline and group management in classrooms.* Melbourne, Florida: Krieger Publishing.

Lasley, T. (1981). Classroom misbheavior: Some field observations. *The High School Journal, Vol. 64, No. 4,* pp. 142-149.

Moskowitz, G., and J.L. Hayman (1976). Success strategies of inner-city teachers: A year long study. *The Journal of Educational Research, Vol. 69, No. 8,* pp. 283-289.

Accountability

Emmer, E., and C. Evertson (1980). Effective management at the beginning of the school year in junior high classes. Paper presented at the American Educational Research Association Meeting, Boston, March.

Fisher, C.W., et al. (1981). Teaching behavior, academic learning time, and student achievement. An Overview. *Journal of Classroom Interaction, Vol. 17, No. 1,* Winter, pp. 2-15.

Location Factor

Adams, R.S., and B.J. Biddle (1970). *Realities of teaching: Explorations with video tape.* New York: Holt, Rinehart and Winston.

Krontz, P.J., and T.R. Risley (1972). The organization of group care environments: Behavioral ecology in the classroom. Paper presented at the meeting of the American Psychological Association, September.

Rist, R.C. (1970). Student social class and teacher expectations: The self-fulfilling prophecy in ghetto education. *Harvard Educational Review, Vol. 40,* pp. 411-451.

Schwebel, A.J., and D.L. Cherlin (1972). Physical and social distancing in teacher-pupil relationships. *Journal of Educational Psychology,* December, pp. 543-550.

Van Houten, R., et al. (1982). An analysis of some variables influencing the effectiveness of reprimands. *Journal of Applied Behavior Analysis, Vol. 15,* pp. 65-83.

Weinstein, C.S. (1979). The physical environment of the school: A review of the research. *Review of Educational Research*, Fall, p. 598.

Rules

Association for Supervision and Curriculum Development (1984). *ASCD update*, ASCD, May.

Emmer, E., and C. Evertson (1980). Effective management at the beginning of the school year in junior high classes. Paper presented at the American Educational Research Association meeting, Boston, March.

Lasley, T. (1981). Research perspectives on classroom management. *Journal of Teacher Education, Vol. 32, No. 2*, pp. 14-17.

Testing and Grading

Freeman, D., et al. (1980). *The fourth grade mathematics curriculum as inferred from textbooks and tests*. Institute for Research on Teaching Report #82. East Lansing: Michigan State University.

Gage, N.L., and D.C. Berliner (1984). *Educational psychology* (3rd ed.). Boston: Houghton Mifflin.

Van Houton, R., and D. Lai Fatt (1981). The effects of public posting of high school biology test performance. *Education and Treatment of Children, Vol. 4*, pp. 217-226.

Van Houten, R. and J. Van Houten (1977). The performance feedback system in the special education classroom: An analysis of public posting and peer comments. *Behavior Therapy, Vol. 8*, pp. 366-376.

Feedback

Fisher, C.W., et al. (1978). *Teaching behavior, academic learning time and student achievement*. Final Report of Phase III-B, Beginning Teacher Evaluation Study, Technical Report V-1. San Francisco, California: Far West Laboratory for Educational Research and Development.

Gage, N.L., and D.C. Berliner (1984). *Educational Psychology* (3rd ed.). Boston: Houghton Mifflin.

Kulik, J.A., and C.C. Kulik (1979). College teaching. In P.L. Peterson and H.J. Walberg (eds.), *Research on teaching concepts, findings, and implications*. Berkeley, California: McCutchan.

Time on Task

American Association of School Administrators (1982). *Time-on-task: Using instructional time more effectively.* Arlington, Virginia: American Association of School Administrations.

Fisher, C.W., et al. (1978). *Teaching behavior, academic learning time and student achievement.* Final Report of Phase III-B, Beginning Teacher Evaluation Study, Technical Report V-1. San Francisco, California: Far West Laboratory for Educational Research and Development.

Justiz, M.J. (1984). It's time to make every minute count. *Phi Delta Kappan,* March, pp. 483-485.

Rossmiller, R.A. (1982). Managing school resources to improve student achievement. Paper presented at the State Superintendent Conference for District Administrators, Madison, Wisconsin, September.

Stallings, J. (1980). Allocated academic learning time revisited, or beyond time on task. *Educational Researcher,* December, pp. 11-16.

Chapter 4

Brandt, R. (1985). On teaching and supervising: A conversation with Madeline Hunter. *Educational Leadership,* February, pp. 61-66.

Goodlad, J.I. (1984). *A place called school: Prospects for the future.* New York: McGraw-Hill.

Karweit, N.L. (1983). Time on task: A research review. United States National Institute of education, Grant No. NIE-E-80-0113. Center for Social Organization of Schools, John Hopkins University, Baltimore, Maryland.

Research for Better Schools, Inc. (1981) ASCD action lab 34—time-on-task: A systematic approach for improving instruction. Research for Better Schools, Inc., 444 North Third Street, Philadelphia, PA 19123.

Strother, D.B. (ed.) (1984). *Time and Learning.* Bloomington, Indiana: Phi Delta Kappa Center on Evaluation, Development, and Research (CEDR).

Chapter 5

Emmer, E.T., et al. (1982). *Organizing and managing the junior high classroom.* Research and Development Report No. 6151. The Research and Development Center for Teacher Education, The University of Texas at Austin.

Chapter 6

Alvord, D.J., and L.W. Glass (1974). Relationships between academic achievement and self-concept. *Science Education, Vol. 58, No. 2,* pp. 175-179.

Becker, W.C., S. Engelmann, and D.R. Thomas (1971). *Teaching: A course in applied psychology.* Chicago: Science Research Associates.

Boules, A. (ed.) (1981). *Crossroads: A handbook for effective classroom management.* Oklahoma City: Oklahoma State Department of Education.

Buckley, N.K., and H.M. Walker (1978). *Modifying classroom behavior.* Champaign, Illinois: Research Press.

Charles, C.M. (1981). *Building classroom discipline.* New York: Longman.

―――― (1983). *Elementary classroom management.* New York: Longman.

―――― (1985). *Building classroom discipline: From models to practice.* New York: Longman.

Curwin, R.L., and A.N. Mendler (1980). *The discipline book: A complete guide to school and classroom management.* Reston, Virginia: Reston Publishing.

Emmer, E.T., et al. (1984) *Classroom management for secondary teachers.* Englewood Cliffs, New Jersey: Prentice-Hall.

Evertson, C.M., et al. (1981). *Organizing and managing the elementary school classroom.* The Research and Development Center for Teacher Education, The University of Texas at Austin.

Ginott, H. (1972). *Teacher and child.* New York: Avon Books.

Jones, F.H. (1979). The gentle art of classroom discipline. *National Elementary Principal, Vol. 58,* pp. 26-32.

Knapp, M.L. (1972). *Nonverbal communication in human interaction.*

New York: Holt, Rinehart and Winston.

Kounin, J. (1970). *Discipline and group management in the classroom.* New York: Holt, Rinehart and Winston.

Paine, S.C., et al. (1983). *Structuring your classroom for academic success.* Champaign, Illinois: Research Press.

Project T.E.A.C.H. (n.d.). *An integrated composite of successful teaching practices.* Westwood, New Jersey: Performance Learning Systems.

Rinne, C.H. (1982). Low profile classroom controls. *Phi Delta Kappan*, September, pp. 52-54.

Scheflen, A.E. (1972). *Body language and the social order.* Englewood Cliffs, New Jersey: Prentice-Hall.

Wallen, C.J., and L.L. Wallen (1978). *Effective classroom management.* Boston: Allyn and Bacon.

Chapter 7

Appleton, N. (1983). *Cultural pluralism in education.* New York: Longman.

Banks, J.A. (1974). Cultural pluralism and the schools. *Leadership, Vol. 32, No. 3*, December, pp. 163-166.

Carducci, D.J., and J.B. Carducci (1984). *The caring classroom.* Palo Alto, California: Bull Publishing Company.

Charles, C.M. (1981). *Building classroom discipline.* New York: Longman.

Curwin, R.L., and A.N. Mendler (1980). *The discipline book: A complete guide to school and classroom management.* Reston, Virginia: Reston Publishing.

Data Research, Inc. (1987). *1987 deskbook encyclopedia of American school law.* Rosemount, Minnesota: Data Research, Inc., pp. 154, 486.

Dreikurs, R., B.B. Grunwald, and F.C. Pepper (1982). *Maintaining sanity in the classroom.* New York: Harper and Row.

Emmer, E.T., et al. (1984). *Classroom management for secondary teachers.* Englewood Cliffs, New Jersey: Prentice-Hall.

Evertson, C.M., et al. (1981). *Organizing and managing the elementary school classroom.* The University of Texas at Austin: The Research and Development Center for Teacher Education.

Gatti, R.D., and D.J. Gatti (1975). *Encyclopedia dictionary of school law.* West Nyack, New York: Parker Publishing.

Hummel, D.L., and C.W. Humes (1984). *Pupil services: Development, coordination, and administration.* New York: Macmillan.

Hummel, K. (1981). Classroom management: Absentee arbiter. *Early Years*, October, pp. 32-33.

Kaercher, D. (1984). The discipline problem in our schools: What's happening? Schultz, F. (ed.), *Education 84/85.* Guilford, Connecticut: The Dushin Publishing Group.

Lemlech, J.D. (1979). *Classroom management.* New York: Harper and Row.

Lightfoot, A. (1978). *Urban education in social perspective.* Chicago, Illinois: Rand McNally.

Martin, R.J. (1981). Coping with excuses. *Learning,* January, pp. 84-85.

Ozark Community Mental Health Center (1985). *Ozark center.* Joplin, Missouri: Ozark Community Mental Health Center.

Paine, S.C., et al. (1983). *Structuring your classroom for academic success.* Champaign, Illinois: Research Press.

Pasternak, M.G. (1979). *Helping kids learn multi-cultural concepts.* Champaign, Illinois: Research Press.

Sloane, H.N. (1976). *Classroom management: Remediation and prevention.* New York: John Wiley.

Walker, J.E., and T.M. Shea (1984). *Behavior management: A practical approach for educators.* St. Louis, Missouri: Times Mirror/Mosby College Publishing.

Wallen, C.J., and L.L. Wallen (1978). *Effective classroom management.* Boston: Allyn and Bacon.

Watchtower Bible and Tract Society (1983). *School and Jehovah's witnesses.* Brooklyn, New York: Watchtower Bible and Tract Society.

Zintz, M. (1969). *Education across cultures.* Dubuque, Iowa: Kendall and Hunt.

Appendices

Bradley, E.K., Jr. (1970). *Intraclass sociability grouping in secondary schools—supporting theory and functional design.* Doctoral dissertation, University of Pittsburgh.

Buckley, N.K., and H.M. Walker (1978). *Modifying classroom behavior.* Champaign, Illinois: Research Press.

Canter, L. (1979). *Assertive discipline: Competency based guidelines and resource materials.* Los Angeles: Canter and Associates.

Charles, C.M. (1983). *Elementary classroom management.* New York: Longman.

Crossroads: A handbook for effective management (1981). Oklahoma State Department of Education.

Dickerson, D., et al. (1974). Let the cards do the talking—A teacher parent communication program. *Teaching exceptional children, Vol. 4, No. 4*, pp. 170-178.

Draper, K. (1984). How am I ever going to combat this class? *The Directive Teacher, Vol. 6, No. 2*, Summer/Fall, 14. Copyright, 1984, NCEMMH, The Ohio State University.

Dunn, R., and K. Dunn (1978). *Teaching students through their individual learning styles: A practical approach.* Reston, Virginia: Prentice-Hall.

Evertson, C.M., et al. (1981). *Organizing and managing the elementary school classroom.* Austin, Texas: The Research and Development Center for Teacher Education, The University of Texas.

Fox, K. (1985). Classroom auction as a bonus for students and teachers. *Missouri Schools,* Missouri Department of Elementary and Secondary Education, February-March, p. 13.

Marwood, L., F. McMullen, and D.H. Murray (1986). Learnball league: Teacher-to-teacher staff development. *Educational Leadership,* February, pp. 56-58.

Runge, A., J. Walker, and T.M. Shea (1975). *Teaching exceptional children.* Reston, Virginia: The Council for Exceptional Children, Vol. 7, No. 3, pp. 91-92.

Sneed, J.P. (1983). The MYTEAM learnball league. *Delta Kappa Gamma Bulletin, Vol. 50, No. 1,* Fall, pp. 9-14.

U.S. Department of Education (1986). *What works: Schools without drugs.* Washington, D.C.: U.S. Department of Education.

Walker, J.E., and T.M. Shea (1984). *Behavior management: A practical approach for educators.* St. Louis, Missouri: Times Mirror/Mosby College Publishing.

Index